PSALM 119 FOR LIFE

PSALM 119
FOR LIFE

LIVING TODAY IN THE LIGHT OF THE WORD

Hywel R. Jones

 BOOKS

EP BOOKS
Faverdale North, Darlington, DL3 0PH, England

e-mail: sales@epbooks.org

EP BOOKS US
P. O. Box 614, Carlisle, PA 17013, USA

e-mail: usasales@epbooks.org

web: http://www.epbooks.org

First published 2009

British Library Cataloguing in Publication Data available

ISBN 13 978 0 85234 703 4   ISBN 0 85234 703 0

Printed and bound in the UK by the MPG Books Group

These expository studies began life as devotional addresses in the Chapel of Westminster Seminary, California.

I am grateful for the goodwill of my colleagues, who gave me more than a fair share of opportunities to minister God's Word on Tuesday mornings. This fuller treatment of the 'Great Psalm' is therefore dedicated to them and their ongoing ministry 'for Christ, his gospel and his church':

Steve Baugh, Scott Clark, Bryan Estelle, Bob Godfrey, Mike Horton, Dennis Johnson, Peter Jones, Zach Keele, Joel Kim, Julius Kim, Jim Renihan, Bob Strimple, David Vandrunen and Joshua Van Ee.

CONTENTS

INTRODUCTION TO PSALM 119

When he preached through the book of Psalms, St Augustine omitted Psalm 119, and when asked to expound it he refused. The length of the psalm was a factor in his decision, but what weighed more with him was its depth, which he claimed was 'fathomable by few', himself included. When he eventually agreed to do so he explained his former reluctance by saying, 'As often as I began to reflect upon it, it always exceeded the utmost stretch of my powers. For in proportion as it seemeth more open, so much the more deep doth it appear to me; so that I cannot show how deep it is.' What he meant by 'more open' was that the psalm's language[1] was straightforward and not characterized by any of the obvious difficulties presented by other psalms. Indeed, so much was this the case for him that he said that the psalm seemed 'not to need an expositor, but only a reader and a listener'.[2]

Why then did he comment on it? Was it just a case of yielding to pressure from others, or of his deciding not to leave unfinished a task that was almost complete? It was neither. The explanation that he gave for treating the psalm is worth pondering. He was concerned that 'in the assemblies of the church [Christians should] not be defrauded of the comprehension of the Psalm, by the singing of which, as much as by that of others, they are wont to be charmed'.

Aware of how the mind can go to sleep when words are set
to music (as, for example, with Psalm 23 sung to the tune
Crimond), he resolved to preach through the psalm so that
the people of God might benefit from understanding its
profound content. Since his day many others have done so
too for the edification of God's people and their growth in
grace.[3]

In recent years Psalm 119 has been given more serious
attention by Old Testament scholars than in the earlier
decades of the twentieth century.[4] One such example is Will
Soll's published dissertation that contains such helpful and
stimulating information on both the literary form of this
psalm and the possible historical occasion for it.[5] Aware that
scholars had treated it in a very dismissive way,[6] he began by
repeating Augustine's comment about the ordinariness of
the psalm and said, 'The psalm poses no major textual or
linguistic difficulties. We have a good idea what the individual words and the individual verses mean.' But he then
added something that Augustine would never have said,
namely, 'And we have no idea why anyone would compose a
Psalm like this.'[7] Attention needs therefore to be given to
the content and purpose of Psalm 119 in relation to Christians and the church. That is what this book seeks to do.

In this introduction a foundation will be provided for the
comment that follows on each of the sections of the psalm.
The English Standard Version will be used for this purpose,
but any preferred alternatives, or rearrangement of the text,
will be indicated by the use of square brackets, or by an
appropriate comment in the course of the exposition.

The language of the psalm

We begin with Augustine's description of Psalm 119 as being
'more open' than others. Such ordinariness of vocabulary is
a conspicuous example of the way in which the Lord

accommodates himself to his people in Holy Scripture. Calvin made the following remark when he preached on this very psalm:

> The will and purpose of the Holy Ghost is to make us to feel and understand that which before I have declared; to wit that the doctrine herein contained, is not only set down for great Clerks which have gone to school for ten or twenty years: but also for the most simple: to the end none should pretend any excuse of ignorance.[8]

By 'none' Calvin was thinking of each member of his congregation, and that chimes well with the use of the first-person singular pronoun which is such a feature of this poem. Apart from the opening general statement, the poem is constructed around 'I' and 'you' because true religion is a personal relationship with the Lord. What is more, the disclosures which the psalmist makes speak *of* the heart and *to* the heart. Calvin's well-known comment on the Psalter applies accurately to this particular psalm. In his commentary he wrote that this book was 'the anatomy of all the parts of the soul, for not an affection will anyone find in himself whose image is not reflected in this mirror. All the griefs, sorrows, fears, misgivings, hopes, cares, anxieties, in short all the disquieting emotions with which the minds of men are wont to be agitated, the Holy Spirit hath here pictured exactly.'[9]

This psalm can therefore be described as having a 'time-less' quality, but only in the sense that it transcends the time and place of its composition (rather than that it does not have one) and speaks so naturally to the church of the Lord Jesus Christ in any age and culture. And, assuming for a moment that it focuses attention on the characteristics of true piety or 'spirituality', who can deny its pressing relevance? The wide gap between God's revealed truth and man's religions (both ancient and ad hoc) is being rapidly closed in many strands of contemporary Christianity. This convergence is traceable in no small measure to the way in which the church (unlike the psalmist here) has moved Holy Scripture to the margins of its own confession and proclamation, worship and witness. The sufficiency of the Word of God for the whole life of the church of the Lord Jesus Christ and of the Christian believer is a vital matter (see 1 Tim. 3:15-16; 2 Tim. 3:16-17).

The form of the psalm

It is a well-known fact that the psalmist used the letters of the Hebrew alphabet as a skeleton for his poem. He assigned one consonant to each section of it in turn, and then opened each line of that section with a word beginning with that consonant. This feature is shown in some English translations by the shape of that consonant being printed above the relevant section as well as its name.

Psalm 119 is therefore an acrostic poem. The word 'acrostic' is a literary term that refers to whatever begins a line of poetry or a sub-part of it, whether a letter or a word.[10] There are other poems in the Psalter that exhibit this feature, namely, Psalms 9 – 10 together; 25; 34; 37; 111 – 112 and 145.[11] But Psalm 119 is the most developed of them all, combining lament (as in Ps. 25), a hymn (as in Ps. 111; 145) and a wisdom song (as in Ps. 112).This is partly why it has been termed 'the Great Psalm'.

Having adopted an alphabetical structure, the poet could have used as many lines as there are consonants in the Hebrew language — that is, twenty-two — as is done in Psalms 25 and 34. It is also true that he could have used some slight variation in the number of lines, as in Psalms 9 – 10 and 37, or a multiple of twenty-two in half-lines, as in Psalms 111 and 112. But in Psalm 119 we have 176 — an acrostic that is considerably longer than all the others put together. Why did he settle on 176 then — not 154 or 198? It is almost certainly because he used eight different nouns in his poem to refer to God's Word, namely 'law', 'testimonies', 'precepts', 'statutes', 'commandments', 'judgements', 'word' and 'promise'. He therefore gave eight lines (or 'stichs') to each consonant or section, resulting in 176 overall.[12] In his most helpful commentary on the Psalms Derek Kidner wrote aptly and delightfully:

> Like a ring of eight bells, eight synonyms for Scripture dominate the psalm, and the twenty-two stanzas will ring the changes on them. They will do it freely, not with a bell-ringer's elaborate formulae, and they will introduce an occasional extra term.[13]

The poet therefore consecrated his skill to a high purpose. He introduced some variety in his deployment of these synonyms and even the length of his lines. He normally wrote lines that have two parts (couplets), but occasionally used a triplet (see vv. 145, 176). It is as if he wanted to show by this flexibility that God's Word conveys freedom as well as consistency (v. 89).

By way of analogy we may think of a sampler — the kind that used only to be available in antique shops. In these a young girl would produce a rural scene with numbers and letters added and perhaps a text of Scripture too, and then append her name and age. By this means she would be saying that she was numerate, literate, had useful skills in homemaking and that she was also religious. The psalmist is striving to show the riches of God's word for human life. He therefore employs the richness of human language and in doing so expresses God's word in man's words, elevating human speech in the process.

Just as letters are needed to construct words that are essential for relationships and activities between human beings (see the Tower of Babel for negative proof), so it is between man and God, or rather between God and man. Letters are basic to words that God deigns to use in order to speak to his people. As the creator of man's organs of thought and speech, he communicates his will to man so that human beings may think about what he has said to them and talk to him about it as they also work for him in his world. Psalm 119 is therefore God's true word to man and also man's proper reply to him. It is conversation with God or, better, communion and co-operation with him. Kidner wrote:

> This giant among the psalms shows the full flower-ing of that 'delight ... in the law of the Lord' which is described in Psalm 1, and gives its personal witness to the many-sided qualities of Scripture praised in Psalm 19:7ff.[14]

By a striking coincidence in numbering, Psalms 1, 19 and 119 focus attention specifically on the law of the Lord.[15] Psalm 1 shows how it divides people into two groups, the godly and the ungodly, describing the 'walk and talk' of each. Psalm 19 focuses on two kinds of divine 'speech', namely God's self-disclosure via the universe and supremely via his law — and it closes with godly 'walk and talk' by way of response (vv. 12-14). Psalm 119 combines the word and deeds of the Lord with 'the walk and talk' of the godly — but in the world of the ungodly.

The authorship of the psalm

Like Proverbs, the book of Psalms is a composite production — only more so! It includes individual poems and ones previously collected either according to 'authorship' (e.g. those of Asaph or Korah) or occasion (e.g. the 'Songs of Ascent'). The reliability of the data in the titles that exist has been strenuously challenged, particularly those that relate to David, but I am content to take them at face value.[16] They are included in the canonical text and David is designated as 'the sweet psalmist of Israel' (see 2 Sam. 23:1).

Psalm 119 does not have any kind of superscription, and so we have no information about its authorship or the occasion of its composition. Even so, there has been a long and unanimous tradition in the church, both East and West, that ascribes it to David. This is certainly not impossible given, firstly, the similarity between its content and spirit and those psalms that bear David's name; and, secondly, the fact that Acts 4 ascribes Psalm 2 to him although it is 'anonymous'. However, it does labour under the difficulty of having to explain why his name should have been omitted if the psalm were in fact his composition. After all, the superscriptions to several psalms in Book 5 do contain his name, namely Psalms 108 – 110 and 138 – 145. Why then should it have been omitted from Psalm 119 if he were indeed its author?

There is, however, something that is more important to explore than an authorial connection between Psalm 119 and King David *individually*. It is whether there is a connection between the psalm and the monarchy in Israel as an institution. This is because Israel's monarchy was not a human convention that was based either on popular choice (as was the case with King Saul) or a social contract between king and people. It had a theocratic character because it was founded on the Lord's covenant with David (see 2 Sam. 7:8-17) and it provided for a dynasty that would issue in the universal and endless reign of the Messiah over the church and the world. It was thoroughly theocratic and eschatological in character. Every descendant of David would as a consequence typify the Messiah, whether by way of limited similarity, or even specific contrast. I would therefore suggest that it is more important to ask, '*What* was the author-poet?' rather than 'Who was he?' In particular, could he have been a king? I think so.

There are three main reasons for connecting this psalm with a Davidic king. The first is thematic. It lies in the connection between the law and kingship. Deuteronomy 17:14-20 is the definitive text on this point. It makes clear that Israel was not permitted to have the kind of king that the nations had. Instead her king was to provide himself with a duly certified copy ('book) of 'this law' of God which he was to read 'all the days of his life' and keep 'so that he [might] continue long in his kingdom, he and his children, in Israel'. The extent of 'the law' referred to in this text is a matter of debate, but it clearly includes more than is found in this section of Deuteronomy. Why not therefore the whole of Deuteronomy? There is no good reason to deny this probability. Israel's kings were therefore to submit to God's rule and to rule for God. This applied first to Moses, the founder of the theocracy, and he commanded Joshua, his successor, in this way (see Josh. 1:7-8). We have a striking example of this with the coronation of Joash after the purge of the Davidic house by Athaliah. In 2 Kings 11:12 we read:

> Then [Jehoiada the priest] brought out the king's son and put the crown on him and gave him the testimony. And they proclaimed him king and anointed him, and they clapped their hands and said, 'Long live the king!'

The 'testimony' is a reference to the law of the Lord that was to be the focus and framework for kingly rule. This is also the dominant theme of Psalm 119.

Secondly, there is a striking correspondence between the psalm and monarchy passages with regard to the terms used for this law. As has been mentioned, one of the most distinctive features of Psalm 119 is that it uses a number of synonyms for the law of God, eight in all. David uses six of them ('statutes', 'commandments', 'judgements', 'testimonies', 'law' and 'word') in his farewell address to Solomon (see 1 Kings 2:3-4, NKJV) and the Lord also uses them in his address to Solomon when the temple was completed (see 1 Kings 9:4-7).

Thirdly, the same expression is used to describe the supreme objective of the psalmist and the thoroughness of the obedience required of the king. Six times in Psalm 119 the words 'with all my heart' appear and this expression is widespread in Deuteronomy. Although its use there is with reference to the people, there is an emphasis on 'the heart' in the portion of chapter 17 that deals with the king and the law. There its use is somewhat negative with reference to the heart being 'turned away' or 'lifted up', both of which lead to disobedience to 'the commandment'. But there is something positive implied because the king was to read the law himself so that 'he [might] learn to fear the LORD his God' (v. 19). In King Solomon's prayer at the consecration of the temple the expression occurs with reference to the people as a whole, including of course the king. In 2 Kings 23:3 King Josiah uses it as he reconsecrates himself to the Lord in connection with the reformation that he instituted in the light of the rediscovery of the 'Book of the Covenant':

> And the king stood by the pillar and made a covenant before the LORD, to walk after the LORD and to keep his commandments and his testimonies and his statutes with all his heart and all his soul, to perform the words of this covenant that were written in this book. And all the people joined in the covenant.

Clearly, obedience to the law of God that was both heartfelt and wholehearted was required of the king, and not only the people. This is everywhere present in Psalm 119.

There are also some extra details in Psalm 119 that mesh easily with 2 Samuel 7 and the history of the monarchy, and so support a royal identification. They are the psalmist's frequent mention of his need for 'life' (for example vv. 25, 149), and of his enemies of various kinds, including 'princes' (vv. 23, 161). There is room for debate as to what the psalmist had in mind by a petition for 'life' and, as we shall see, there are good grounds for arguing that the immediate setting in which each such plea is found should be allowed a determining voice in answering that question. But the possibility that it is at least connected with the continuance of a king's reign over against his foes, or in spite of his own unworthiness, should not be excluded. David records such a request over against his foes in Psalm 21:4-8, and Psalm 89 is the 'prophetic' explanation of the institution and collapse of the monarchy.

A significant parallel to this is found in Lamentations 4:20. There a spokesman for the people, most probably Jeremiah, declared after the fall of Jerusalem to the Babylonians in 586 BC:

> The breath of our nostrils, the LORD's anointed,
>   was captured in their pits,[7]
> of whom we [had] said, 'Under his shadow
>   we shall live among the nations.'

The Davidic king was a guarantee of the Lord's covenant relationship with the people and a means of 'life' for them. His loss, coupled with the destruction of the temple and the exile of the people, resulted in the nation's 'death', depicted in the vision of 'a valley of many, dry bones' (Ezek. 37:1-17). The author of Psalm 119 is a king who did not want that to happen in his day.

There is also some difficulty in being precise as to the nationality of these 'foes'. Are they Israelite or not? Soll argues for their being from the surrounding nations, and in support of this he points to the psalmist's description of himself as a stranger (vv. 19, 54) — that is, someone who does not belong in the land where he lives. He then proceeds to argue for an exilic context for Psalm 119 and for Jehoiachin as its author. But there is no need for such a literalistic understanding of 'stranger', which, as he acknowledges, could have a metaphorical sense. David used the word in this sense when he was impressed with the transience of life (see Ps. 39:12; 1 Chr. 29:15) and, in addition, was he not opposed from within Israel both by Saul and his own son, Absalom, becoming a fugitive in his own land?[18]

The purpose of these remarks, however, is not to argue that David was the author of Psalm 119, but that it was one of his descendants who composed it. The Lord had promised David that he would have a descendant who would 'build a house' for the Lord's name and whose kingly throne would be 'established for ever'. Psalm 119 is therefore the expression of a descendant of David who believed this. (Would not King Josiah be a good candidate, especially as verse 9 refers to 'a young man'? See also v. 99 and 2 Chr. 34 – 35.)[19] But it chiefly relates to David's 'greater Son', the Lord Jesus Christ, who kept the law of the Lord for the good of his people and who enables them, in union with him, to live in accord with it in his kingdom.

We shall therefore consider Psalm 119 in that twofold way. First, we shall see it in the context of an Israelite king in his kingdom, and then view it with regard to the Lord Jesus Christ and his church and subjects. Using this line of interpretation, Andrew Bonar wrote in his book entitled *Christ and His Church in the Book of Psalms*, 'We cannot err far, therefore, if ... we keep "our left eye" on David, while we have our right eye full of Christ.'[20]

Augustine speaks in similar vein in commenting on Psalm 58. He says that 'the voice of Christ and the church' is heard in it.[21] The most important thing to bear in mind in considering it is not David personally, but David typically.

Jesus Christ, the seed of David and the Son of God (Rom.
1:3), is the Lord's anointed and he, raised from death's
prison, will ever be 'the breath of life' in the 'nostrils' of his
people (see Gen. 2:7; John 11:25-26).

The placement of Psalm 119

Considerable attention has been given of late to the arrangement of psalms in our Psalter. This is not an entirely
new insight. In 1850 J. A. Alexander of Princeton made an
interesting comment on this subject by saying:

> The arrangement of the psalms in the collection is
> by no means so unmeaning and fortuitous as may at
> first sight seem to be the case, but that in many
> instances at least, a reason may be found for the juxta-
> position, in resemblance or identity of subject or
> historical occasion, or in some remarkable coinci-
> dence of general form or of particular expression.[22]

But seeing a psalm in relation to its predecessors and successors and in relation to the particular book of the Psalter
in which it is found is an approach that has been given
considerable attention of late.[23]

Applying this to Psalm 119 enables the following synthe-
sis to be offered. Psalm 119 comes between two collections
of poems. Preceding it we have six poems (Ps. 113 – 118) that
are songs of praise for deliverance. They were all used at the
annual Passover — two songs before the meal and four after
it. Kidner comments with his usual succinctness and
lucidity:

> Only the second of them (114) speaks directly of the
> Exodus but the theme of raising the downtrodden (113)
> and the note of corporate praise (115), personal thanks-
> giving (116), world vision (117) and festal procession

(118) make it an appropriate series to mark the salvation which began in Egypt and will spread to the nations.[24]

Following it are fifteen psalms that are called 'Songs of Ascent' (Psalms 120 – 134). They relate to pilgrims making their way to Jerusalem for one or other of the stated feasts. Six of these are connected with kingship too; four are by David, one by Solomon and a fifth concentrates on the life and reign of David.

Surveying the movement of thought in Psalms 113 – 134, we find an arrangement that bears all the marks of deliberate intent. We are required to believe in a redemptive work, then proceed to a sanctifying word and finally join a worshipping pilgrim people. Although this is depicted in terms of the old covenant, they of course have their counterpart and fulfilment in the work of Christ, the Word of God and the worship of the church.

Conclusion

Psalm 119 is therefore most worthy of being called 'the Great Psalm', and not only because of its complex form but its central theme, which is that the Word of God provides 'all things [necessary] to life and godliness' (2 Peter 1:3). It anticipates true Christianity in every way and every Christian should give it his, or her, serious and regular attention. It is therefore a spiritual as well as a literary *tour de force*. Remarkable poetic skill is wedded to singular piety in order to send a message to the people of God about the Word of God and the way of the godly — in a fallen world.

Testimonies to Psalm 119

Psalm 119 has been spoken of impressively by so many who have preached on it and written about it. In addition to Augustine, Calvin, Bonar and Kidner, whose comments have been referred to earlier, the following will be of interest and benefit:

Martin Luther

It contains prayers, consolations, doctrines, thanksgivings, and repeats all these with a varied fulness. It is given forth with a deep and blessed intent; namely that by this repetition and fulness, it may invite and exhort us to hear and diligently to treasure up the word of God.[25]

John Calvin

Behold now, how the Lord our God here teacheth us as it were by an ABC a most excellent song amongst the rest, by which we may learn to rule and order our lives, whereby also he exhorteth us to well doing, to comfort us in all our afflictions, to ratify unto us the promises of salvation, to open unto us the gates of his everlasting Kingdom, that we might enter into everlasting life.[26]

Jonathan Edwards

I know of no part of the Holy Scriptures where the nature and evidences of true and sincere godliness are so fully and largely insisted on and delineated as in the 119th Psalm. The psalmist declares his design in the first verses of the psalm, keeps his eye on it all along, and pursues it to the end. The excellency of holiness is represented as the immediate object of a spiritual taste and delight. God's law, that grand expression and emanation of the holiness of God's nature, and prescription of holiness to the creature, is all along represented as the great object of the love, the complacence and rejoicing of the gracious nature which prizes God's commandments above gold...[27]

E. W. Hengstenberg

A characteristic feature of our psalm is the deep conviction that we have nothing to do with human strength in keeping the commandments of God, but that God alone must create the will and the power to perform. The church of God has been convinced of this from the beginning.[28]

Joseph Addison Alexander

There is no psalm in the whole collection which has more the appearance of having been exclusively designed for practical and personal improvement, without any reference to national or even to ecclesiastical relations, than the one before us, which is wholly occupied with praises of God's word or written revelation, as the only source of spiritual strength and comfort, and with prayers for grace to make a profitable use of it.[29]

Charles Bridges

It contains the anatomy of experimental religion, the interior lineaments of the family of God. It is given for the use of believers in all ages, as an excellent touchstone of vital godliness, a touchstone which appears especially needful in this day of profession; not as warranting our confidence in the Saviour, or as constituting in any measure our ground of acceptance with God: but as exciting us to give 'diligence to make our calling and election sure' (2 Peter 1:10) and quicken our sluggish steps in the path of self-denying obedience.[30]

1.
BLESSED AND BLAMELESS

Psalm 119:1-8

[1] Blessed are those whose way is blameless,
    who walk in the law of the LORD!
[2] Blessed are those who keep his testimonies,
    who seek him with their whole heart,
[3] [they] also do no wrong,
    but walk in his ways!
[4] You have commanded your precepts
    to be kept diligently.
[5] Oh that my ways may be steadfast
    in keeping your statutes!
[6] Then I shall not be put to shame,
    having my eyes fixed on all your commandments.
[7] I will praise you with an upright heart,
    when I learn your righteous rules.
[8] I will keep your statutes;
    do not utterly forsake me!

The psalmist opens the first two lines of this section (and of the psalm as a whole) with exactly the same word. Nowhere else does he repeat himself in this way.[1] Evidently, he wants to focus attention on a people who are 'blessed'. This is

reminiscent of the first line of Psalm 1 and the last line of
Psalm 2, which, taken together, describe those who live by
the law of the Lord and who trust in his Messianic king as
those who are blessed indeed. This is an anticipation of the
Beatitudes (cf. Matt. 5:3-12).

The Lord and his law

Throughout this psalm God is referred to as 'the LORD' apart
from one place (v. 115), and even there God's name has the
first-person singular pronoun attached to it. The psalmist is
therefore in no doubt that *his* God is 'the LORD' (see 1 Kings
18:24-39), and it is as such that he regularly addresses him
(see the opening lines of nine of the sections which make up
the psalm and also twelve other uses of the name). What is
the significance of this designation?

The term 'Lord' is printed in two ways in English translations of the Old Testament when it applies to God. This
variation is to indicate which of two different words is used
in the Hebrew text. 'Lord' means 'master, owner or ruler',
whereas 'LORD' is the way in which translators have usually
indicated that the divine name stands in the Hebrew text. It
is always important to take note of this difference whenever
one is reading the Old Testament in order to call to mind
the appropriate meaning in each case.

It is the deliverance of Israel from Egypt that makes clear
the meaning and power of the name 'LORD' although it was
known and used before (see Gen. 4:26). Exodus 3 and 6 are
the chapters that give crucial information with regard to it.
In answer to his request to be told God's name, Moses is
informed that the God of his people's fathers is 'I AM WHO I
AM', abbreviated to 'I AM' (Exod. 3:13-14). Because of the way
in which the tense of a verb is expressed in Hebrew, this can
also be rendered as 'I will be who I will be', and declarations

that encompass both present and future activity had in fact already been made known to Moses (see Exod. 3:6, 12).

There is therefore a twofold dimension to this name. It points to who God is and will be, and to what he has done and will do for his people. Unlike all other 'so-called gods' and 'lords' (1 Cor. 8:5-6; Ps. 115:1-8), he is the 'I AM' — he is alive and his existence is self-derived. Similarly, his activity is self-determined and he is the 'I will [be]' (see Exod. 33:19; Rom. 9:15, where sovereign, gracious activity is described). In the present and the future God will benefit his people because he is in covenant with them, as he was with their founding fathers (Exod. 3:15). 'LORD' is his 'his name for ever', and that is how they identify themselves and address him (see Gen. 4:26; Isa. 44:5).[2]

Genesis uses the word *'elohim'* ('God') where God's creative acts are recorded (see Gen. 1:1 – 2:3), but 'LORD *elohim'* where his governance of all his creation is in view (see Gen. 2:4 – 3:24), an administration of law and grace, judgement and salvation (see James 4:12). 'God' stands for Creator; 'LORD' is Judge and Saviour. 'The LORD' in this psalm is none other than the 'God and Father of our Lord Jesus Christ', and that is how we should think as we consider all it says about him.

Eight nouns are used with regularity in this psalm for the Lord's will for his people. (Five of them also appear in Ps. 19:7-14.) In the ESV they are rendered by seven English terms, namely 'law', 'testimonies', 'precepts', 'statutes', 'commandments', 'rules' and 'word'. The numerical discrepancy between eight in the Hebrew and seven in the English is the result of the fact that two of the Hebrew nouns both mean 'word'. One of these can also mean 'promise', and that is more suitable in some lines of the poem. Translations also differ with regard to some of the other terms.

More important than such variations, however, is the question of how all eight nouns relate to each other. Are they synonyms or not? If they are, is any distinction in meaning possible between them? If they are different, can there be any common ground between them? These questions are important for a consideration of all that follows.

From the fact that some of the eight terms are plural and others are singular (two of them appear in both forms), we may deduce that neither meaningless repetition nor radical differentiation between them is possible. There are differences to be noted, but there is also a consonance and a harmony, a variety within an overall unity. Law (*torah*) and word (*dabhar*) are both singular. They are the Lord's spoken and written will for his people and include what the other terms signify. 'Testimonies' ('*edhoth*) are solemn declarations. They are expressive of the idea of bearing witness, as is made clear by the fact that the Book of the Law was placed beside the ark 'for a witness', or, literally, a 'testimony' (Deut. 31:26). 'Precepts' (*piqqudhim*) is a term that is almost unique to this psalm. They are detailed requirements that result from official oversight such as Joseph was given in house of Potiphar (Gen. 39:4). 'Statutes' (*huqqim*) have an abiding quality; the noun comes from a verb meaning to engrave. 'Commandments' (*mitswoth*) are characterized by authority. 'Rules' (*mishpatim*) are just judgements ('rulings' might be a better rendering). 'Promise' ('*imrah*) is intended to encourage and be a basis for expectation (see vv. 38, 41).

The historical setting in which all these have meaning and force is the era of the Sinaitic covenant. In some sense they can all be described as 'law', which is the dominant term in the poem, being used in the first line and more often than any other (twenty-five times). But it is covenant law that is in view, which means the divinely determined framework within which the Lord's relationship with his people, and theirs with him, can flourish (see Exod. 19:4-6). On the basis of his deliverance of them, they were more than obligated to obey his will — and those who did so 'happily' and gratefully, like the psalmist, were blessed indeed.

No legalism is therefore being countenanced or advocated by this term 'law', and that is shown by the fact that 'promise' is the next in terms of frequency. Law and promise form the way that God governs and guides his people into increasing fellowship with him, both individually and corporately. Law directs, positively and negatively, and promise supports and restores. This is so in the new-covenant era as well. Jesus, the mediator of the new covenant, laid down commandments for those who trust in him. He summed up the Ten Commandments (on which all Israelite laws were based) by the two great laws of love (Matt. 22:35-40) so that they can now be called 'the law of Christ' (Gal. 6:2) and he provides his followers with gracious aid (Heb. 4:16).

The Lord and his people

Like the Beatitudes, the opening three lines of this poem are in the third person plural. The psalmist is announcing that the blessedness of the Lord's people is bound up with a life that consists of '[walking] in the law of the LORD' and '[keeping] his testimonies ... precepts ... [and] statutes'. One or other of the metaphors of 'walking' and 'keeping' occurs in each of the first five lines of this section and then again in the last. Both of these verbs are used in the New Testament as well. More is involved here than a mere knowledge of the law of the Lord (cf. Matt. 7:21-27; Rom. 2:17-29; James 1:22-25).

This is a summary of true piety in Old and New Testament terms. Zechariah and Elizabeth are described as 'walking blamelessly in all the commandments and statutes of the Lord' (Luke 1:6). Jesus said to his disciples in the upper room, 'If you know these things, blessed ['happy', KJV] are you if you do them' (John 13:17), and 'If you love me, you will keep my commandments' (John 14:15). The same

combination of ideas is found in 1 John 2:3-8, where Christians are to 'walk' in accord with Christ's 'word' — i.e. his
'commandments' — and also his example, for they are 'to
walk in the same way in which he walked'. The apostle Paul
uses the word 'walk' much more frequently than 'keep' with
reference to Christians generally, and 'keep', or 'guard',
rather than 'walk', with regard to Christian ministers in
particular (see Eph. 4:1; 1 Tim. 6:20). Obedience to the Lord's
will is therefore the hallmark of true piety, and the godly
recognize that it is demanded, but also know that it is
desired. Christians are to live in ways devoid of what is
blameworthy, not only in terms of God's law, but even by
human standards (1 Cor. 5:1).

There are two Hebrew words for 'blessed' in this psalm.
One is used with reference to the Lord (v. 12) as the one who
is worthy of praise and prayer. A different word is used here,
one that is more accurately translated by the word 'happy'.
It is often used in the Old Testament, is echoed in the New
and appears twenty-six times in the Psalter.[3] Two things are
to be noted about it.

First, it is always used in the plural number, and that is
an idiom that indicates excellence or intensity. No ordinary
or limited happiness is therefore in view, but one that is
immeasurable and incomparable, and the plural functions
as an exclamation. The NASB has 'how happy' and that is a
good way of conveying the spirit of the term as well as its
sense. 'How fortunate' has been suggested as an alternative,[4]
but that is quite unsuitable because it leaves room for the
thought that the blessedness of the godly is not the result of
a divine purpose or action.

Secondly, it always introduces either a privilege that has
been conferred — for example, having the Lord as one's God
(see Ps. 144:15; 146:5) — or a character that is being formed
(see Ps. 1:1; 41:1).[5] This connection between privilege and
character means that the kind of happiness that is in view is
the result of human beings having been blessed by the Lord.

It does not come from 'Lady Luck'. It is the people of the
Lord, who is himself to be 'blessed', that are 'happy'. He has
lavished blessings on them in Jesus Christ and they are more
than 'happy' to praise and serve him in return (Eph. 1:3-14).

The word 'blameless' (ESV) translates a Hebrew word
that is used for sacrifices which are without blemish in
relation to the requirements of God's law (e.g. Exod. 12:5)
and it acquires a moral sense for what is acceptable to him.
It does not mean 'sinless', but a life that is rounded out, in
contrast to what is in part — whether that is due to super-
ficiality or insincerity. 'Blameless' means that no fault is
evident in a person's life which demonstrates a lack of
'wholehearted' devotion to the Lord (v. 2) or a proneness to
consistent wrongdoing that attracts blame from others and
from God.[6] The word is combined with 'upright', which
means straight (see v. 7; cf. Job 1:1), and with a word connected with the word for 'peace' in the books of Kings and
Chronicles.

Although the law determines what is blameless, the word
has a relational character. This is because the law's requirements are the Lord's own 'ways' (v. 3) in which he will walk
in fellowship with his people who walk with him, rather
than contrary to them (see Lev. 26; Rev. 2 – 3). Such thor-
ough obedience is neither unnecessary nor excessive. It is no
less than the Lord requires (v. 4). His law is a transcript of
his character, and his desire is that his people should be
increasingly blessed by being conformed to him (see Lev.
11:44; 1 Peter 1:16).

And those who are blessed by knowing the Lord make it
their desire as well! What the Lord demands is no less than
what the godly desire and determine to pursue. The authority with which he makes his law known is matched by the
earnestness of the psalmist to uphold it unswervingly. The
word translated 'steadfast' is the same one as is used in verse
90 for the '[establishing of] the earth so that it stands fast',
and so the psalmist wants the word on which God's throne

rests to be set up in his heart so as 'to take every thought captive to obey' Christ (see 2 Cor. 10:5). This aim is not merely so that he may not attract blame, but that he may never be inwardly ashamed when he looks into God's Word.

In fellowship with the Lord the psalmist resolves to praise the Lord wholeheartedly and to keep his statutes. He is also glad to do this for he has been blessed, but he does not trust in the strength of his resolve to accomplish his solemn desire. He invokes the Lord's aid, and in particular asks that he might be 'schooled' in the Lord's judgements and not left to his own strength (vv. 7, 8).

These truths and convictions are an introduction to all that follows. They formed the mind-set of the psalmist as he looked upward to the Lord and forward to the coming of the Messiah. They should characterize every Christian as he or she looks back to Jesus Christ and forward to his return.

2.
FROM GENERATION TO GENERATION

Psalm 119:9-16

⁹ How can a young man keep his way pure?
   By guarding it according to your word.
¹⁰ With my whole heart I seek you;
   let me not wander from your commandments!
¹¹ I have stored up your word in my heart,
   that I might not sin against you.
¹² Blessed are you, O LORD;
   teach me your statutes!
¹³ With my lips I declare
   all the rules of your mouth.
¹⁴ In the way of your testimonies I delight
   as much as in all riches.
¹⁵ I will meditate on your precepts
   and fix my eyes on your ways.
¹⁶ I will delight in your statutes;
   I will not forget your word.

This psalm has been described as 'a young person's psalm' because of the question with which the section opens.[1] The psalmist is probably referring to himself here, but that cannot be proved because he does not speak in the first person singular, as he does in the rest of the section. But even if he is not referring to himself, the question he poses is not theoretical. It strikes a note of urgency because of the importance of young men for the future of the people of God. In all cultures youth is the period of life that holds out such promise for the young themselves and for the family and community to which they belong. This was especially so in Israel, where the family was the cornerstone of the nation's relationship with the Lord, and young males in particular would exercise leadership in the next generation. By mentioning the need for purity the psalmist indicates that youth is a time that is fraught with great danger and that he is concerned for the young.

Such concern is voiced in several ways in the Old Testament. In the law, it is enshrined in the Fifth Commandment: 'Honour your father and your mother, that your days may be long in the land that the LORD your God is giving you' (Exod. 20:12). This command is in the second person singular and so is the duty of each one in Israel who has living parents. There is also the fact that rebellious and blasphemous behaviour on the part of any young man was a capital offence. In wisdom literature, the king was to address his son (Prov. 1 – 7; 23) in much the same way as the psalmist speaks here. But it was also a matter for prayer because one aspect of the happiness of those whose 'God [was] the LORD' (Ps. 144:15) was that, having informed their children of his saving deeds and instructed them in his ways, they could ask him:

> May our sons in their youth
>   be like plants full grown,
> our daughters like corner pillars
>   cut for the structure of a palace
>
> (Ps. 144:12).

So much of the history of Israel revolved around its 'young' men, whether for good or ill. On the one hand there were Joseph, David, Josiah and Daniel and his friends, but on the other Saul, Absalom and Rehoboam's associates who exerted considerable influence in the break-up of the kingdom after the death of Solomon (see 1 Kings 12:8). (Peer-group pressure is no new phenomenon!) The death of the young, whether male or female, but particularly male, was a colossal tragedy (Ps. 78:63), as in the case of the destruction of Jerusalem and the exile (see Lam. 1:15, 18; 2:21; 5:13, 14). This was a clear indication that the Lord had withdrawn his promised blessing. And why did he do so? It was because his people did not heed his word (see Zech. 7:8-14), the very thing that the psalmist is speaking of here.

The same is true with regard to both the Lord Jesus and his church. At twelve years of age Jesus became a 'son of the law',[2] but showed himself a master of it by endorsing and expounding it (see Mark 7:9-23; John 19:26-27; Eph. 6:1-4). He began his ministry when he was young in the eyes of others (Luke 3:23; John 8:57) and he died while still a young man 'holy, innocent, unstained' (Heb. 7:26). Furthermore, Saul was a young man when he was humbled by the Lord Jesus Christ (see Acts 7:58; 8:1; 22:20) and he, now known as Paul, later sent young Timothy to Ephesus. Whatever Timothy's age might or might not have been is not a critical factor; purity was. 'Keep yourself pure' from 'youthful lusts' was the apostolic injunction (1 Tim. 4:12; 5:22; 2 Tim. 2:22, NKJV), and it still is.

In the rest of this section the psalmist provides an answer to the pressing question he raises. It consists of two main parts.

By guarding it according to God's word

The psalmist has already desired that his ways might be steadfast in the Lord's ways (vv. 3, 5) and he now makes clear that for that to happen he must be on his 'guard', on sentry duty as it were. Youth is not a time for thoughtless, let alone reckless, conduct, but for coming to terms with oneself and taking one's place in society and among the people of God. And that is not easy, because young persons soon realize that their world is not what they would like it to be and also that they themselves are not what they would like to be — and that often the two are related. How to find a way for oneself through this fallen world when one is not pure oneself is therefore a colossal question. But there is no better time for asking it than when one is young (Eccles. 12:1) and Scripture provides a suitable answer: 'It is good for a man that he bear the yoke in his youth' (Lam. 3: 27).

Youth is therefore a time for serious reflection about what 'one's way of life' is going to be like. Life is precious and the way in which one lives is serious. Neither is to be treated lightly but 'guarded' well, just as Adam was to guard the temple-shrine of Eden (see Gen. 2:15). The 'gates of Mansoul' are to be defended.[3] The way to do this is to take one's life to the word of the Lord, or the reverse, as the psalmist strongly advises and does himself, given what he goes on to say. Instead of keeping the law at arm's length, he brings it before and beside himself so that he might not stray from the Lord's way and sin against him (vv. 10, 11). That is what Adam and Eve failed to do.

By seeking the Lord with his whole heart

This provides the setting in which all the rest follows. Two things should be noted here.

The first is that in the Bible 'the heart' is not a synonym for the emotions. It contains 'the springs of life' that affect thought and desire, speech and action (Prov. 4:23-27; 23:26). The heart is the person in miniature.

Secondly, the psalmist strikes such a fine correlation here between the word and the Lord (vv. 10-12), one that is often not followed because God and his word are either disconnected or to all intents and purposes identified. God is so much above his word, and yet his word reveals him as nothing else does. He is therefore to be sought by means of it, or in accord with it, and certainly not apart from it or in contradiction of it. He is the full counterpart of his self-revelation, promises and precepts, and under his blessing they produce conformity to him. As at creation his word produced his image, so in re-creation his word restores it. Using God's word with reference to himself, the psalmist says that he will walk with him in his ways (vv. 1-3) and not 'wander' from it or sin 'against God' (vv. 10-11). He therefore asks the Lord to teach him all that the law contains so that he might indeed do it. The psalmist wants the Lord to enrol him in his school, to make him his disciple. What will that involve?

The psalmist's aims

All that follows this general reply is an unfolding of what is entailed in this 'guarding' and 'seeking'. The psalmist settles on specific aims. They are all related to the Word of God and to prayer for the Lord's presence and help (see vv. 10, 12) — as much to the one as to the other because piety is working, not wishing. But working without praying is unproductive because it lacks the Lord's blessing (see Ps. 127). Jesus said, 'Without me you can do nothing' (John 15:5, NKJV) and he made the sanctification of his people a matter of prayer to his Father (John 17:17).

There are four goals that the psalmist sets himself with regard to the Lord's words and ways. We shall consider them in pairs.

'Storing up' and 'declaring'

The first of these is in order to the other. The word that is translated 'store up' is used for Jochebed's action with regard to the infant Moses on account of Pharaoh's edict (Exod. 2:2), an act carried out more to preserve than to conceal because it was done in faith (see Heb. 11:23). The same can be said of the psalmist's activity because he intends to make public what the Lord has said and done, and not to conceal it. 'Storing up' is necessarily preparatory to 'declaring' because it is 'out of the abundance of the heart' that 'the mouth speaks' (Matt. 12:34).

This emphasis on 'storing up in the heart' may be in contrast to having the law merely on the doorposts and gates of houses and on the forehead and arm (see Deut. 6:4-9; Isa. 29:13). It was in these terms that Jesus exposed his generation (Mark 7:6). The 'heart' certainly includes the mind, even the memory — and memorization of Scripture is an all-too-rare practice nowadays. To 'declare' means to speak to others, friend and foe alike, and the psalmist refers to both (see vv. 21, 63). What has come from God's mouth is now uttered by human lips (see also Matt. 12:34-37).

'Delighting' and 'meditating'

The connection between these is twofold because delight is expressed both before and after the decision to meditate. The delight that is taken in the word fuels meditation, and that in turn heightens the pleasure and the profit. David says, 'As I mused, the fire burned; then I spoke with my tongue' (Ps. 39:3). The delight that is spoken of here is measured against the joy that riches bring. Later on the psalmist will say that he prefers the law to riches (v. 72) and to 'fine gold' (v. 127), and later still that it can be compared to finding great spoil (v. 162). Here his point is that his joy in the law of the Lord is not one whit less than all the joys that the greatest riches can bring — and that is no mean evaluation!

His meditation is close and intense. He focuses attention on the precepts of the law — a copy of the law must have been before him and his eyes are riveted on what is recorded of the Lord's ways with his people there. But the verb can also mean doing this aloud — that is, by repetition — and that is frequently mentioned (see vv. 23, 27, 48, 78, 148; cf. Luke 2:19, 51). It is by means of meditation on what he has already said that the Lord will speak to his people and school them in his paths.

In the middle of this section the psalmist blesses the Lord. 'To bless' is to speak well of, and even to benefit. The Lord has spoken and done what is good to his people. He is their great benefactor; they are his beneficiaries. But the good they do to him is by way of praise, obedience and the pursuit of purity. This is no more and no less than what is appropriate. But even for that they are in need of his gracious aid — and that is so from generation to generation.

3.
SERVING AMONG SCOFFERS

Psalm 119:17-24

[17] Deal bountifully with your servant,
   that I may live and keep your word.
[18] Open my eyes, that I may behold
   wondrous things out of your law.
[19] I am a sojourner on the earth;
   hide not your commandments from me!
[20] My soul is consumed with longing
   for your rules at all times.
[21] You rebuke the insolent, accursed ones,
   who wander from your commandments.
[22] Take away from me scorn and contempt,
   for I have kept your testimonies.
[23] Even though princes sit plotting against me,
   your servant will meditate on your statutes.
[24] Your testimonies are my delight;
   they are my counsellors.

This section contains a new feature. It is the existence and activity of those who oppose the Lord and his people. They compound the psalmist's difficulties because he no longer has only his own weakness with which to contend. We shall consider the content of this section in relation to those adversaries and the psalmist's reactions to them.

The adversaries

They are identified as 'princes', or some of them are. This term can, and does, refer to royalty, both in the surrounding nations and in Israel, but it does not have to be understood in such a narrow sense. It has a wide scope of reference and any official or leader in Israel could be in view (see 1 Chr. 29:6). 'Prince' refers to someone with a position and the power that goes with it — a power that can easily intoxicate with pride, and so often does. This is the detail to bear in mind (see further in v. 161).

Their character

Their character is summed up by one word, which is translated 'insolent'. Wherever this word is used in the Old Testament it always describes an attitude that is opposed to the Lord and his people. Its essence is summed up in Proverbs 21:24: '"Scoffer" is the name of the arrogant, haughty man who acts with arrogant pride,' in contrast to the preceding verses, which refer to someone who pursues righteousness and controls his own spirit. One illustration of this is in Jeremiah 43:2, where the prophet (no longer a 'young man' in years) meets with leaders whose disposition, manifested in their words and deeds, amounts to insolence. The psalmist was confronted by such people (see vv. 51, 69, 78, 85, 122). An identikit picture of these people can therefore be built up from these details.

Their conduct

With regard to their conduct, they 'wander from [the LORD's] commandments' (v. 21). This means that, like the psalmist, they had been recipients of God's revelation. They were part of the Israel of the day! Although the psalmist has used this expression with regard to himself (see v. 10), wandering from the Lord's commandments was something that he abhorred and sought to prevent becoming fact. That is not so with the 'high and mighty'. They are not only wandering, but have no compunction about doing so, as is shown by their words and deeds against the psalmist.

Their words

Their words are scornful and contemptuous (v. 22). They make him the butt of their reproach and contempt (see v. 39; cf. Ps. 123:3-4), and all on account of his being the Lord's 'servant' (see the psalmist's identification of himself in verses 17 and 23). As a 'servant' of the Lord, the psalmist keeps his 'testimonies' — that is, his words to his people. These scoffers think that their words are more weighty and true than God's words (see Ps. 73:3-9).

Their deeds

Their deeds are specified by the expression, '[they] sit plotting against me' (v. 23). This points to some kind of official process, whether in private (the word 'plotting' points in this direction) or publicly, as in some kind of investigative hearing. Although the opening of verse 23 *could* be translated by 'even though', as in the ESV, the word 'also' is a better translation. No theoretical possibility is being envisaged by the psalmist here; an actual situation is being described.

'The Servant of the Lord', Jesus Christ, experienced such assaults. He was grossly maligned as a blasphemer against God's law, and was tried and condemned as such by the Jewish 'princes'. This was also true of Stephen (see Acts 6:13-14) and the apostle Paul (Acts 22). Something similar has since happened to many Christians. Reviewing the history of Isaac and Ishmael, the apostle Paul declared that 'he who was born according to the flesh persecuted him who was born according to the Spirit' (Gal. 4:29). All this is a reflection of the age-old struggle between 'the seed of the serpent' and 'the seed of the woman' (see Gen. 3:15; Rev. 12:17) that has not yet been terminated — but it will be.

Their judgement

With regard to the judgement that hangs over them, the psalmist calls them 'the accursed ones'. This means that they are under the curse of a broken covenant (see Deut. 27; Gal. 3:10). Under God's curse they stand in antithesis to those who are 'blessed'. A differentiation is therefore made within the people of God in the Old Testament, as the apostle Paul taught: 'For not all who are descended from Israel belong to Israel, and not all are children of Abraham because they are his offspring' (Rom. 9:6-7).

These scoffers are subject to the divine curse on account of their demeanour and behaviour. This makes clear that the ground of damnation is found in man, whereas the ground of salvation is found in God (see Rom. 9:22-24). God is neither morally indifferent nor partial. His favour is no protection against his wrath if his kindness is despised (Amos 3:2), as is shown by the history of Israel culminating in exile in Babylon (see Deut. 28:15-68). His holy displeasure was first manifested among mankind with the sin of Adam and Eve and their expulsion from the garden of God, but neither that nor the disasters listed in Deuteronomy 28 exhausted its grim meaning and reality. It results in an 'outer darkness' and 'a bottomless pit' where 'there is weeping and gnashing of teeth' for ever. It is depicted in advance in the affliction and isolation of Jesus on the cross, the completely pure 'young man', under the wrath of God (see Deut. 21:23, quoted in Gal. 3:10-13).

In the rest of this section the psalmist responds to this hostility and persecution. He renews his declaration that he is a servant of the Lord, but also acknowledges that he is a 'sojourner on the earth' (or in the land). He makes requests and also rejoices.

The sojourner

It is not necessary to think that the psalmist is outside the land of Judah in order to do justice to this term. All Israelites were described in this way (see Lev. 25:23) and David used similar language at the height of his prestige when he provided Solomon with the plan of the temple, and gifts were given by the leaders and families of Israel towards its construction (see 1 Chr. 29:15). Although 'a sojourner' was not a full Israelite, he was not the same as 'a foreigner'. Both could spend time in Israel, but the sojourner was one who stayed. More than that, he did not bring idol worship with him as the foreigner did (see 1 Kings 11:1-8). The sojourner settled in a land that did not belong to him, just as Israel had done for forty years in Egypt. This was why Israel was to treat the sojourner in a different way from the foreigner (see Deut. 10:19). Christians are also represented as strangers (see 1 Peter 1:1; 2:11).

The sojourner had many privileges, but no land was his, and this gives the clue to the psalmist's description of himself. It is as though he is in a foreign land because of the way in which 'princes' are living in the Lord's land in defiance of his law. This is why he describes his spirit as broken with longing and asks the Lord not to conceal his commandments from him (vv. 19-20). He desires to see the Lord's words being honoured and obeyed.

His requests

These arise out of this need and they provide an answer to it on the personal level. He asks the Lord to deal bountifully with him in terms of his free and full goodness, his grace (see v. 65). In particular he asks for life (v. 17), light (v. 18) and liberty from reproach (v. 22).

In view of his threatening circumstances, which become worse as the psalm proceeds (see v. 95), it is not possible to exclude from this request for life the idea of continued existence. There is nothing unworthy in being apprehensive on that score (see 2 Cor. 1:8-11). Even so, it is not life in itself that he craves, but life for a purpose, namely, that he might continue to serve the Lord and keep his commandments on earth. He is not only asking for breath, but strength — and strength of mind and spirit to persevere in faith in a hostile environment (see Phil. 1:19-26).

What would help greatly in this respect is a fresh and fuller discovery of the riches of God's word (v. 27) and to be free of scorn. 'Wondrous things' are God's acts of judgement and deliverance, not some deeply hidden truth that the words of God's law cannot convey (see v. 130). He is surrounded by those who do not truly understand God's words and deeds (see 1 Cor. 2:14) and so he desires to see these things in a new light. But he believes that he cannot contemplate the wonders in God's law without the Lord's aid. He needs to have his eyes 'uncovered' so that he sees, or understands, what he actually reads (see v. 27). This is a confession both of inadequacy and inability. What he has seen and the resources he has are not sufficient in and of themselves to enable him to see more, and by his own effort he cannot remove the dimness of his own soul. He needs the Lord to be his teacher.

To be the object of incessant scorn and scheming is oppressive. It can become unbearable. This request arises out of the experience that David calls 'the strife of tongues'

(see Ps. 31:20). To have them fall silent would be a consol-
ation, and that is what he prays for. It was the frequent
experience of the Lord at the hands of the scribes and
Pharisees, and the apostle Paul counsels that prayer should
be offered for such quietness to enable open and effective
Christian conduct (see 1 Tim. 2:1-3).

But the psalmist has not lost all joy. He still knows that
'wondrous things' are contained in the law of the Lord and
also that the Lord will deal well with him. In the closing
verse of the section there is something that must not be
overlooked. He declares that he has counsellors who advise
him as to how he should cope with his adversaries, with
their craft and clamour. Those confidants are the Lord's own
testimonies, or the Lord himself who speaks through them
to those who meditate on them (see Isa. 30:21).

4.
BROAD AND NARROW WAYS

Psalm 119:25-32

[25] My soul clings to the dust;
  give me life according to your word!
[26] When I told of my ways, you answered me;
  teach me your statutes!
[27] Make me understand the way of your precepts,
  and I will meditate on your wondrous works.
[28] My soul melts away for sorrow;
  strengthen me according to your word!
[29] Put false ways far from me
  and graciously teach me your law!
[30] I have chosen the way of faithfulness;
  I set your rules before me.
[31] I cling to your testimonies, O LORD;
  let me not be put to shame!
[32] I will run in the way of your commandments
  when you enlarge my heart!

Five of the lines in this section begin with the same Hebrew word ('way'), and not just the same consonant. This is due to the constraints of the acrostic arrangement and the fact that relatively few Hebrew words begin with this letter. Even so, it should not be thought that the psalmist had no higher purpose in his choice of words than maintaining an art form. He consecrated an art form to the service of truth, and not the reverse. 'Art for art's sake' was not his motto.

The noun 'way' is used five times in these eight lines; once in the plural (v. 26) and four times in the singular, and without any major difference in sense between them. In addition to its primary meaning the word is used metaphorically for the habits of animals and the customs of human beings (see Prov. 30:19) on the one hand, and also for the demands of the Lord and his dealings with his people (v. 27) on the other. It is in this metaphorical sense that it is used here because the psalmist is relating his way(s) to the Lord's way(s). He records how they can diverge and what results when that happens, but also what happens when they come together again. We shall use each of these as headings for our study.

On his own way

Twice the psalmist refers to his own ways in this section (see vv. 26, 29) and twice to his 'soul' (vv. 25, 28). There is a connection between these, and it is that the character of his ways reflects the condition of his soul. 'Soul' is a synonym for 'breath' and 'being' — that is, the life of a person. It therefore stands for mind and spirit, everything that animates the body. By 'my soul cleaves to the dust' (NASB) and it 'melts ... for [i.e., weeps on account of] sorrow' he means that inwardly he is both abased and enfeebled. His vitality is destroyed. He is not explicit about the cause of this death-like experience, but he gives something of a hint of it (v. 29). This verse needs to be carefully weighed in terms of a more accurate translation and analysis of his trouble.

The translation

The ESV translation (printed at the head of the chapter) has failed to render the opening of verse 29 properly and to show the way in which it is balanced by the opening of verse 30. Verse 29 opens with an idiomatic expression that means '[the] way of falsehood' and verse 30 similarly with '[the] way of faithfulness'. In each case the paired nouns are closely connected so as to make one idea. Both expressions are given emphasis by their position in the line and they are obviously in contrast with each other. But this is obscured in the ESV by the first being turned into a plural and rendered 'false ways'.[1]

The psalmist is thinking here about two ways spread out before the people of God. The one falsifies and distorts the covenant of the Lord, while the other is in keeping with it and manifests it. They are the equivalent of the broad road and the narrow way (see Matt. 7:13-14). We may also call to mind how it was customary in the early days of the church to refer to Christians as followers of 'the/this way' (see Acts 9:2; 19:9, 23; 22:4; 24:14, 22).

The trouble

The psalmist is troubled about this 'way of falsehood' and he asks the Lord to 'turn [it] away' from him. But he does so as one who has 'chosen the way of faithfulness'. What can he mean? Is he on these two paths at the same time? The answer to that question must be 'No' given what has been said earlier about the words and deeds of those who are 'false' (see v. 21) who contribute towards this grief by their scorning and scheming. But there is another contributory factor. The psalmist himself has already referred to his need for steadfastness in the Lord's statutes (v. 5; see also 1 Cor. 15:58).

Such a potent mix goes a good way towards explaining the psalmist's trouble. His foes, who are on the way of falsehood, are near at hand and he himself is not as firmly and consistently on the way of faithfulness as he wants to be. He is weak. His 'ways' (v. 26) show that he has forgotten the Lord's commands and wandered from them (see vv. 10, 16), and that is what has produced this dust-and-ashes experience. The psalmist is not 'double-minded' (v. 113). In the dust he 'clings' to the Lord's 'testimonies' (vv. 25, 31) and depends on the Lord's grace (v. 29). Jesus was sorrowful in soul, even unto death, in the Garden of Gethsemane, but that was because he was taking the place of his straying sheep (of whom the psalmist was one — see v. 176) and was about to bear their due punishment.

Towards the Lord's way

These verses are a prayer, as is the case with many sections of this psalm and with the psalm as a whole. The psalmist turns to the Lord confidently with confession and supplication in order that he might learn his ways (see vv. 1-3).

Confession

In verse 26 he refers to recounting his ways to the Lord. This must include confession of sin, given the context, although the usual vocabulary associated with sin is not used. What the psalmist writes goes to the heart of the matter because genuine confession is person to person, the offender to the offended, just as Jesus depicted the return of the prodigal with the words: 'I will arise and go to my father, and I will say to him ...' (Luke 15:18; see also Hosea 14:1-3). He therefore makes that soul-journey in confidence of being favourably answered (v. 26) because his God is 'the LORD', the one who hears and answers prayer (Exod. 3:7-9).

Supplication

The psalmist is aware that he needs 'life' (v. 25), understanding (v. 27) and strength (v. 28), and he asks for them boldly. He has deprived himself of these soul-blessings and returns to the Lord with expectation that he will have them restored.

Life

This context guides us as to how the verb 'give life' should be understood. Is it 'preserve', which means 'keep alive' and is often understood as having a physical reference, or is it 'revive', which means 'to restore to life' and has a spiritual dimension? In this section such a distinction cannot be pressed too hard in view of the fact that the psalmist is under threat (v. 23) as well as in gloom and grief. But non-acknowledgement of sin is also connected with psychological and even physical effects such as weakness and groaning (see Ps. 32:3-4). The life he is asking for must therefore include 'life in the inner man' (see 2 Cor. 4:16).

Understanding and strength

These are bracketed because they describe the kind of life that the psalmist knows he needs. It is because his ways have diverged from the Lord's ways in some respect(s) that he knows that his understanding is superficial and/or partial. He therefore asks the Lord to 'teach' him (v. 26) so that he might 'understand' (v. 27) and meditate on the 'wondrous works' of the Lord — that is, his saving acts. Perhaps he had lost sight of the gospel, which provides the context in which the many demands of the law are to be set by the redeemed, or he had failed to see something that was 'false' in its true colours. His 'sins' would therefore come into the category of sins of ignorance, as distinct from presumptuous sins (cf. Lev. 4; Num. 15). This request for a deeper understanding of the Lord's statutes is made in dependence on the Lord's grace and favour (v. 29).

The life that the psalmist asks for is therefore in accord with the Lord's word (v. 25) and works (v. 27). It is not an end in itself. He has chosen the way of faithfulness not merely because of its attractive appeal to the mind, but so that he might walk according to its judgements, discerning right from wrong and becoming more and more faithful to the Lord. He therefore asks for strength to live in the light of what he knows.

On the Lord's way

This is alluded to in the final line of this section. It contains a surprise. Given what the psalmist has said, we might expect him to speak about walking in the Lord's ways (see v. 3). Instead he speaks of running in them — a striking contrast to wandering! To run is a metaphor for energetic activity (see Rom. 9:16). This verb is used in only one other place in the Old Testament with regard to God's ways. It occurs at the end of Isaiah 40 as a description for steady and ongoing activity as a result of waiting on the Lord for the fulfilment of his promise of comfort (see Isa. 40:1-3, 29-31). Isaiah 40 is a prediction of the return from Babylon, which is also a type of the Messianic age, as is 'the enlarging of the heart'.

Comments have already been made on the significance of the term 'heart' in the Old Testament (see chapter 2). It includes the mind and the will with its affections. The verb 'enlarge' with which it is connected evokes the prospect of better days for Israel as she comes into the promised land (see Deut. 12:20). That promise eventually opens out into the new-covenant era (see Isa. 54:2-3; 60:5). The 'enlarge-ment of the heart' is therefore the antitype of the extension of Israel's territory. It is better than 'a land flowing with milk and honey'. The psalmist expects that he will run in the Lord's ways *when* that happens. It is the alternative to 'being faint and weary' and exceeds the strength of youth (just like a soaring eagle).

At this point we need to remember that, although there is a continuing thread of truth and experience between the Old and the New Testaments which must not be lost sight of, there is also a difference to note that is most significant. It relates to the Holy Spirit and how his working is regulated by the amount of truth that has been disclosed. The more truth that is disclosed, the greater the understanding and power that are communicated to those who believe it. The Spirit of God is referred to in the Old Testament in connection with creation (see Gen. 1:2), with the enrichment and administration of all that is created (see Ps. 104:30) and also with regard to redemption, both objectively and subjectively, both corporately and individually (see Isa. 63:11; Ps. 143:10). But his work in the believer as a result of Christ's accomplished atonement, resurrection from the dead and exaltation to the right hand of God produces life more abundant still.

So this section is an anticipation of that reviving that comes to the Lord's wayward people. Displaying his saving work to them again, he pardons and cleanses his humbled people, answers their prayers, teaches them his word, renews their consecration and enlarges their zeal so that they become more fervent in his cause than they have previously been.

5.
LIFE FOR THE HEART

Psalm 119:33-40

³³ Teach me, O LORD, the way of your statutes;
   and I will keep it to the end.
³⁴ Give me understanding, that I may keep your law
   and observe it with my whole heart.
³⁵ Lead me in the path of your commandments,
   for I delight in it.
³⁶ Incline my heart to your testimonies,
   and not to selfish gain!
³⁷ Turn my eyes from looking at worthless things;
   and give me life in your ways.
³⁸ Confirm to your servant your promise,
   that you may be feared.
³⁹ Turn away the reproach that I dread,
   for your rules are good.
⁴⁰ Behold, I long for your precepts;
   in your righteousness give me life!

The first lines of this section continue the theme of the previous one with the mention of 'way' and 'the heart'. In both the psalmist makes a request to the Lord for 'life'. This shows that a continuity of thought may be present between

one section of this poem and the next. Here it is an aware-
ness that life is needed and that the Lord is the source of
this life and that he will give it. We shall therefore use this
focus on 'life' as the organizing theme for comment on this
section.

The need for life

What kind of life is the psalmist asking for? The verb he
uses in verse 37 is one that he employs a number of times in
his poem and it is rendered in different ways in our English
translations — 'renew', 'restore' or 'revive'. Strictly speaking,
each of these words is accurate, but perhaps none of them is
wholly serviceable because each has become associated with
movements in the life of the church. What must not happen
is that the emphases and practices of those movements
should be read back into this psalm as an interpretation of
what the psalmist is saying. He is not endorsing any (and
every) renewal, restoration or revival *movement*. Indeed
what he is saying needs to be taken seriously by them all.

The best translation of the Hebrew verb is therefore by
way of some neutral but meaningful expression. The KJV has
'quicken', and that is fine but it is archaic. The ESV has 'give
me life', and that is much better. Beginning with this line of
thought, we can go on to explore the rest of this section.
From the fact that the psalmist is talking to the Lord it
should be noted that in one sense he already possesses 'life',
yet at the same time he is aware that he needs 'life' and that
the life he needs comes from the Lord.

There is another time-honoured word that begins with
the prefix 're-' which is attested in this particular prayer, and
that is 'regeneration'. The fact that the psalmist 'delights' in
the commands of God (v. 35) signifies that he has been given
'a new heart, and a new spirit' (Ezek. 36:26). Those who are
spiritually dead do not, indeed cannot, seek after God (Rom.

3:11) and cannot please God (Rom. 8:8), but those who have
received life from above (see John 3:3) will seek more of that
life from its giver. The psalmist has been born again (John
3:3, 5). Regeneration occurred in the Old Testament as truly
as in the New, but it was not understood as clearly. In
answer to Peter's severely limited understanding, the Lord
had to inform his disciples that they (with the exception of
Judas Iscariot) had been bathed and so only needed to be
washed subsequently (see John 13:10; 15:3).

The 'kind of death'

In a fallen world it is always a kind of death that gives rise to
the need for a related kind of life. What kind of 'death',
then, was the psalmist conscious of and concerned about?
Was it illness, or waywardness, or vulnerability to foes, or
just spiritual decline? What does he say in this section that
relates to this?

In the two verses where he pleads for life (vv. 37, 40)
there is nothing about a threatening illness, but his use of
the term 'reproach' (v. 39) gives a clue that foes were present
and active. (That takes us back to verses 21-23 and points to
continuity between this section and its *two* predecessors —
not to mention its successor! — see vv. 42, 46). Perhaps the
whole psalm has a single focus, namely the need of the
godly (Israelite) among the ungodly, which would transfer
with ease to new-covenant times and to the church in the
world.

But there is a word in verse 37 that the psalmist has not
used before. It is connected with his request for life and is
therefore a description of the kind of death that he is deal-
ing with. The word is translated 'worthless things' in the
ESV, but it is a singular noun in Hebrew and has a collective
function. It sums up and describes the thoughts and plans,
values and desires of fallen human beings. It is a synonym of

the word that is used so often in Ecclesiastes for life 'under the sun' — in other words, life in a fallen world. But it also has a more narrow reference, and that is in connection with idols (Ps. 24:4; Jer. 18:15). In verse 36 the term that is rendered 'selfish gain' (ESV) is also closely associated with the idea of 'covetousness', which in turn is connected with idolatry (Col. 3:5). This is reminiscent of the sin of Achan (Josh. 7) and anticipates that of Demas (2 Tim. 4:10).

So the kind of death that was troubling the psalmist was the 'course of [the] world' (Eph. 2:2) of his own day and generation. It included the religious as well as the social and was all that was false and futile, deceptive and deadening. God owns the world, but Satan has set up a kingdom within it which is opposed to God and the godly. Though his reign has been put down in their hearts he still has a foothold in their 'flesh', and that includes not only words and deeds but also thoughts and desires. They must resist him and mortify 'the deeds of the body'. It is hand-to-hand combat — kill or be killed (see Rom. 6:12-19; Eph. 4:17-32; Col. 3:1-17). That was so in the Old Testament and the New, and it is so today.

The kind of life

The psalmist has mentioned 'life' once before (v. 17) and there it was understood by way of a desire for continued existence as a 'pilgrim and a stranger' in his environment (1 Peter 2:11). Here the life he desires is described more fully and from two angles. It is a life that 'inclines the heart' and that comes from God's 'righteousness'.

Inclining the heart

The verb that is used in verse 36 means 'to stretch out' or 'to bend'. It is commonly employed with reference to a hand or a staff. But what does it mean in connection with the heart?

Is it something different from verse 32, where the psalmist spoke of the heart being 'enlarged'? Probably not, because both verbs are used in a figurative sense and are connected with an extension of grateful obedience. No greater mistake could be made in thinking about the word 'heart', in both the Old and the New Testaments, than to identify it with the emotions. It is the person in miniature, the source of character and conduct. It contains 'the springs of life' (Prov. 4:23).

To have the heart inclined is therefore to have the whole person directed (see v. 112). In what follows there is by implication a reference to 'feet' in verse 35 and to 'eyes' in verse 37; the latter is a metaphor for desires (cf. 'the lust of the eyes' — 1 John 2:16, NKJV). The primary reference, however, is to the mind, to the understanding (v. 34), because nothing affects character and conduct so much as thoughts. When the Lord Jesus catalogued the manifold wickedness of the heart, 'evil thoughts' are what he mentioned first (Mark 7:21; see also Gen. 6:5). Consequently to 'bend', or 'extend', the heart begins with the teaching of the mind (vv. 33, 34).

But the heart is no more to be identified with the mind than with the emotions or the will. It includes them all, and it is God's gracious regenerative work — the giving of a new heart — that integrates them again in a new creation. The mind fires the emotions and both are expressed in the will. The result is that the feet (deeds) are directed steadily into God's ways and the eyes (desires) are set on his words with delight (vv. 34, 35, 40) and longing. The inclining of the heart includes the enlightening of the mind, the inflaming of the affections and the liberating of the will — that is, the sanctification of the believer.

The Lord's righteousness

The psalmist prays for all this with confidence because he is convinced that God will note (see 'behold' in verse 40) and hear his fervent longing for 'life in [God's] ways'. His assurance that it will be so is based on God's 'promise' (v. 38) and his 'righteousness' (v. 40; see also vv. 137-144). This combination of terms points to the covenant as the framework in which God will do what is right to those who are right with him and give what he has promised to those who trust him. He provides what he promises, which in this case is life for the soul in times of need. He does so, not because the psalmist is sinless or perfect, but because God is 'the LORD'. He is the covenant Redeemer who keeps safe those who trust in him and provides for their every need as they keep his commandments.

This is so for every Christian. As believers in the Lord Jesus Christ, they have God as their heavenly Father (John 20:17). He will work all things together for their good (Rom. 8:28), providing for their every need (Rom. 8:32; Phil. 4:19). He will 'never leave or forsake [them]' (Heb. 13:5-6).

6.
DESIRING AND DETERMINED

Psalm 119:41-48

⁴¹ Let your steadfast love come to me, O LORD,
>   your salvation according to your promise;
⁴² then shall I have an answer for him who taunts me,
>   for I trust in your word.
⁴³ And take not the word of truth utterly out of my mouth,
>   for my hope is in your rules.
⁴⁴ I will keep your law continually,
>   for ever and ever,
⁴⁵ and I shall walk in a wide place,
>   for I have sought your precepts.
⁴⁶ I will also speak of your testimonies before kings
>   and shall not be put to shame,
⁴⁷ for I find my delight in your commandments,
>   which I love.
⁴⁸ I will lift up my hands towards your commandments,
>   which I love,
>   and I will meditate on your statutes.

Not very many words in Hebrew begin with this consonant (*waw*) and as most of them are names of people or places, they are hardly suitable for a poem with this theme and purpose. The psalmist's palette is therefore somewhat limited. But such are his poetic gifts that this presents him with no great difficulty because the name of the consonant is also a word in itself. It is the most basic conjunction in the Hebrew language. It can have a positive or negative meaning and is usually translated by 'and' or 'but' depending on the context. Variations of the former, such as 'even', 'then', or 'so', are also possible. This conjunction therefore contains a potential variety of meanings.

But it also has another meaning, one that is richly significant. It refers to the hooks of the tabernacle (Exod. 38:28), in which everything was to be made 'according to the pattern shown to Moses on the mount'. That is what this psalm is, and was composed to be — a verbal tabernacle for the Lord and his people to commune with each other (see comment on v. 108).

The psalm's high theme is therefore not endangered by its acrostic pattern, and this is a micro-example of the way that human language cannot present an insuperable obstacle to the infallible and living communication of God's truth. Like small hooks, so every jot and tittle in Scripture contributes to the rearing of that antitype of the tabernacle in the wilderness, namely the church of the Lord Jesus Christ in the world, and the greater tabernacle in heaven.

Theoretically speaking, a translation of each line of this section could begin with either 'but' or 'and'. The sense of each statement, however, makes the word 'but' totally unsuitable because the psalmist is so positive in all that he says, whether it is about the Lord or about himself — and that in spite of the fact that he acknowledges the presence and activity of adversaries! He follows one affirmation with another, beginning each line with a verb irrespective of whether he is speaking of the doings of God or of man. This is an indication that his prayer for more life has been answered. His heart *has* been enlarged. There are no 'ifs and buts' in what he says, and to introduce even one would cause confusion in the thought of every verse and through-out the section as a whole. 'For ever and ever' (v. 44) fills the horizon of his believing mind.

Before we look at the content of this section there is some-thing important to note about the verbs in it. It is not their tenses, but their moods. The mood of a verb describes not only who does the action (subject or object), but also how that action is to be done — for example, the imperative mood conveys a command. Here the verbs are either jussives ('let your ...') or cohortatives ('and I will ...'). Jussive verbs express earnest desire (vv. 41-42); cohortative verbs express confident resolve (vv. 43-48). We shall consider these two sub-sections, namely verses 41-42 and 43-48, under the headings of 'desire' and 'determination'.

Desire

The connection between verses 41 and 42 does not need to be explained. It is self-evident. We therefore take up the first line, which expresses dependence. Every word in it is rich in meaning. Comments have already been made on the name 'LORD' and also on the word 'promise', and they need not be repeated here, but it is not superfluous to stress that the psalmist is not depending on any supposed merit of his own, but wholly on the Lord's mercy. The words 'steadfast love' and 'salvation' make that clear.

'Steadfast love' is a term that combines relationship and obligation. It describes how any two parties should regard and relate to each other because of a bond between them. 'Covenant' is the biblical term for this. It is used with regard to individuals (see 1 Sam. 18:3), tribes (Gen. 21:32), a king and his subjects (2 Kings 11:17), or the closest human relationship of mutual obligation — that of husband and wife (Mal. 2:14). Carrying all these dimensions, 'steadfast love' describes how the Lord relates to his people to whom he has committed

himself, and how they should consequently relate to him.
The classic example of it in the Old Testament is found in
the book of Hosea, where its enduring character shines out
so clearly against the background of infidelity.

The psalmist is therefore addressing 'the LORD', his
covenant partner, when he mentions a foe (v. 42) and makes
a request for 'salvation'. The Lord's deliverance of his people
from Egypt is evidently in his mind. Such a remembrance
not only informs his petition, it also strengthens it, giving it
urgency and confidence. The covenant and its promises
provide both the stimulus and the basis for his prayer —
and that is so for Christians too. Jesus has accomplished the
'exodus' (Luke 9:31) and sealed the covenant with his own
blood, and so prayer 'in his name' for 'more life' is bound to
be heard. Grace upon grace has been procured and it cannot
fail to be bestowed (see Heb. 4:14-16).

The psalmist is therefore pleading the covenant in this
request (see Ps. 74:10). He is not content with a past demon-
stration of covenant love, but is asking for a further manifestation of it to him in his present need. He asks that
'steadfast love' may 'come' to him so that he may be able to
answer 'the one' who reproaches him. Elsewhere he uses the
plural to refer to his adversaries (see vv. 21, 23), but here he
employs the noun in the singular number. While this could
be a way of summing them all up in one, it could, on the
other hand, specify a particular individual who was their
ringleader. In either case, with a fresh assurance of the
Lord's favour, the psalmist can face and answer his oppo-
nent, refuting lies and testifying to the truth (see Heb.
13:5-6; 1 John 2:1-3).

Scorn and reproach cut and kill. 'Death and life are in the
power of the tongue' (Prov. 18:21; see also James 3:5-8). The
people of God have often been exposed to the 'strife of
tongues' (Ps. 31:20). The Lord Jesus Christ experienced reproach many times (see Matt. 9:24; Luke 16:14; Mark 15:20, 31),
and so it was with his followers (see Acts 17:18; 23 – 25). But

they witnessed a good confession, as he did (see 1 Tim. 6:13; Acts 4:13; 2 Tim. 4:16-17), aided in accord with his promise (see Mark 13:11-13). But, even if they are not arraigned before authorities, they can be accused by their conscience (1 John 3:20-21). Behind all unjust reproach, derision and accusation is Satan himself, 'the accuser of the brethren' (see Job 1 – 2; Rev. 12:10). But saints overcome him 'by the blood of the Lamb and by the word of their testimony' (Rev. 12:11).

Determination

Desiring that he might always be ready to confess the Lord's 'word of truth', the psalmist prays that it may never be taken from him (v. 43). This negative expression does not imply any doubt concerning the Lord's faithfulness, but is a way of deferring to God's majesty and expressing dependence on him. The word for 'meditate' (v. 48) refers to speaking (or singing) to oneself. With a sense of God's love in his heart, and his word living in his mind, he resolves to do a number of things, all of which can be connected with the role of the king in Israel. These are to keep the law, to testify to it and to worship in accord with it, and every Christian is a king and priest through union with Jesus Christ (Rev. 1:6).

To keep God's law

The basic meaning of this word is to 'guard', so that something may not be lost or taken away. The king was to read the law each day so that his reign and his life might not contradict it.

To testify to it

The 'kings' could be rulers of the surrounding nations. Much of the religious and moral decline in Israel was the result of her kings copying those of the surrounding nations. Such a

desire was partly behind Israel's request for a king (see
1 Sam. 8:5) in contradiction of the Lord's word (see Deut.
17:14-20). But 'princes' are also referred to in much the same
vein (vv. 23, 161), and so perhaps too much weight should
not be put on the meaning 'kings' here. Priests were also to
teach God's law (see Mal. 2:1-9).

To worship in accord with it

The 'lifting up of the hands' is not directly linked with God's
word elsewhere in the Old Testament. When used in a
religious context, it occurs in relation to the sanctuary, and
therefore to worship. Praise of God cannot be excluded from
its scope of reference (see Ps. 63:4; 134:2) but prayer is the
dominant perspective (Ps. 28:2; 1 Tim. 2:8). Lamentations
3:41 makes it clear that the lifting up of the hands is to
express 'the lifting up of the heart'. Desire and delight must
therefore be part of what really lies behind the unusual
expression of lifting up hands 'towards' God's word.

The desires for aid are expressed prior to the resolves
being made, but that does not mean that the psalmist is
bargaining with God, saying in effect, 'If you will, then I
will.' No conditions are mentioned in these verses and such
thinking is the very antithesis of true piety. Instead he is
expressing dependence on divine grace for the accomplish-
ing of all duties and privileges, and confidence in its sufficiency for that purpose. This is therefore an Old Testament
example of what the apostle Paul taught by saying, 'Work
out your own salvation ... for it is God who works in you'
(Phil. 2:12-14). The believer 'works out' because God 'works
in'. All the believer's good resolves and works are the result
of God's grace.

7.
A STRANGER AND A SINGER

Psalm 119:49-56

[49] Remember your word to your servant,
    in which you have made me hope.
[50] This is my comfort in my affliction,
    that your promise gives me life.
[51] The insolent utterly deride me,
    but I do not turn away from your law.
[52] When I [remember your judgements] from of old,
    I take comfort, O LORD.
[53] Hot indignation seizes me because of the wicked,
    who forsake your law.
[54] Your statutes have been my songs
    in the house of my sojourning.
[55] I remember your name in the night, O LORD,
    and keep your law.
[56] This blessing has fallen to me,
    that I have kept your precepts.

As was the case in the previous section, not many words in the Hebrew language begin with this consonant. This time the psalmist chooses a different way to respond to this limitation. He gives prominence to two words and repeats them. The first of these is the word 'remember' (vv. 49, 52, 55) and the second is the demonstrative pronoun or adjective 'this' (vv. 50, 56). Evidently there is something that he does not want to be forgotten. In fact he does not only want it to be remembered by himself (v. 55) but also, and more importantly, by the Lord (v. 49). His double use of 'O LORD' in this section is particularly noteworthy (vv. 52, 55), as is his reference to himself as the Lord's 'servant' (v. 49).

Remembrance

The kind of recollection that is in view here is neither notional nor unproductive, irrespective of whether it relates to the Lord or to the psalmist. When the Lord 'remembers', he does not merely call to mind, but he stretches out his arm. He acts. He puts his covenant promise to his people into operation and provides for them in their need (vv. 49, 50). The Exodus is of course the prime example of this. Remembering his covenant with Abraham, Isaac and Jacob, the Lord delivers their descendants from bondage and into liberty, from hardship into a land flowing with milk and honey (Exod. 6:5-8).

Similarly, when his people remember him they turn to him and call on his name in humble praise, fervent prayer and zealous obedience (Exod. 20:8). When they ask him to remember them, they are therefore asking him to act in accord with his covenant promise (Neh. 13:14, 22, 29, 31). Such acts are his covenant 'judgements' (v. 52, NKJV) by which he saves his people and judges their foes.

Such a recollection of God's redemptive dealings is part and parcel of both the expression and the growth of authentic piety in Holy Scripture. In the Old Testament it lies at the heart of ongoing obedience (Deut. 8; 9) and of worship (Deut. 16:3, 12), whether corporate or individual (Exod. 20:1-17). It is basic to everything in this psalm, and the word is used frequently in the Psalter as a whole. It is also the case in the New Testament, as is made clear by the Lord's Supper, at which believers in the Lord Jesus partake of the benefits of Christ's atoning death by the ministry of the Holy Spirit until he comes again (Luke 22:19; 1 Cor. 11:24-25).

Comfort

But what is it that the psalmist wants to have remembered? What does he have in mind by the word 'this'? In the opening line he makes an oblique reference to it by saying that it is something that the Word of God holds out to him as an object of hope. In the second line he becomes specific. He refers to the comfort that the Lord gave him in a time of affliction and describes that as bringing him 'life' (see discussion of vv. 25-40).

Such a recollection on his part brings him a measure of comfort (v. 52), and that is what is referred to in the first part of verse 56, which, literally rendered, is: 'This I have had.' The second part of that line is: 'I have kept your precepts.' In Hebrew a conjunction joins those two phrases which can mean 'that' (as in the ESV). But it can also mean 'because', and it is that rendering which is to be preferred. The psalmist is therefore remembering something he had as a result of, or in the course of, keeping God's precepts: 'This I have had because I kept your precepts.' Truly 'there is great reward' in keeping God's word (Ps. 19:11). But what he wants is more than a present recollection of past mercies. He wants a repetition, or renewal, of them because it is as though he were not in his own land (v. 54). He wants a mini-Exodus.

A stranger

In the Israel of the psalmist's day there were those who scorned the godly. They were the 'insolent' who, having turned their backs on God and his law (v. 21), regularly derided the psalmist for his believing maintenance of it (vv. 49, 51). This was also the case with other servants of the Lord at other times (e.g. Jer. 20:7-8; Matt. 5:11-12). Indeed, such treatment at the hands of the wicked was predicted of the Messiah himself (Ps. 22:6-8; Mark 10:34) and it was fulfilled both in his living and in his dying (Matt. 9:24; 27:29-31, 39-44). His people are also to endure unjust treatment as meekly as he did, to bless and not to curse, but to leave judgement to God (1 Peter 2:18-25; 3:9-17; 4:12-14; Rom. 12:19-21), and that is what the psalmist does.

But the ongoing opposition he had to endure was all to no avail because he refused to renounce God's name and depart from his law as his foes had done. Instead, by night as well as by day, he is righteously indignant on account of their insolence against the Lord (v. 53). The word that he uses for 'hot indignation' refers to the hot wind that blew from the desert. It is expressive of the all-consuming displeasure of God (Ps. 11:6; Lam. 5:10) and here it describes the psalmist's sense of identification with God in his just judgement. He is not unaffected by their slandering, but he is not moved from his devotion by it — and that is of course true of God as well. God will deride those who have derided him; he will scorn scorners (Ps. 2:4; Prov. 3:34). Even so, the psalmist later records his grief over the wicked (v. 136) and that is something that God does too (Ezek. 33:11). The Lord Jesus Christ wept over Jerusalem (Matt. 23:37-39; Luke 19:41).

The psalmist has already referred to his sense of the transience of life (v. 19) and his use of the word 'house' (v. 54) could therefore be metaphorical (see 2 Cor. 5:1-5). On the other hand, he could be outside Israel himself or be

referring to occasions when that was true of some other
Israelite. King David would be a notable and well-known
example when he had to flee from Saul, or later from Absalom (see 1 Sam. 19 – 31; 2 Sam. 15 – 19; Ps. 3; 63). But wherever the psalmist is (and whoever he is), it is clear that he
knows he is not truly and fully at rest, at home. Life is a
journey for him and it is filled with obstacles and diversions,
but it is by no means joyless.

A singer

The psalmist sings as he goes on his way (v. 54). It is one
thing to talk, but another to sing. Singing is more than
making sounds. It requires spirited activity, whether that is
by way of expressing gladness or lament. For a pilgrim and a
stranger to sing means that, in spite of contrary circumstances, and even experiences, he knows he has something
that is most valuable. In this case it is the 'statutes' of the
Lord.

These are at one and the same time an antidote to the
opposition of the wicked and to the transience of life,
because 'statutes' are characterized by permanence. They
are not subject to alteration when they are challenged and
denied; much less are they annulled or do they lapse into
abeyance. This is because they are the statutes of the Lord
who is not only Saviour, but also sovereign. That is his name
(v. 55). He is the 'I AM/WILL BE THAT I AM/WILL BE'. He
cannot be dethroned by his foes, nor will he disappoint his
people. His promises are true and his precepts are good.
They are therefore fit subjects for spiritual praise. 'The LORD
redeems the soul of his servants, and none of those who
take refuge in him will be condemned' (Ps. 34:22, NASB).

Identifying himself as 'servant' (v. 49), stranger and
singer (v. 54), should the psalmist not be considered as one
of those unnamed individuals in Hebrews 11 who in faith

looked for the comfort and strength of God's grace in their earthly life and pilgrimage? He is among those who constitute 'the great cloud of witnesses' to Christian people. He resembles Bunyan's Christian, albeit before his time, and truly belongs to the communion of saints.

8.
LIVING IN THE LORD'S LOVE

Psalm 119:57-64

[57] The LORD is my portion;
    I promise to keep your words.
[58] I entreat your favour with all my heart;
    be gracious to me according to your promise.
[59] When I think on my ways,
    I turn my feet to your testimonies;
[60] I hasten and do not delay
    to keep your commandments.
[61] Though the cords of the wicked ensnare me,
    I do not forget your law.
[62] At midnight I rise to praise you,
    because of your righteous rules.
[63] I am a companion of all who fear you,
    of those who keep your precepts.
[64] The earth, O LORD, is full of your steadfast love;
    teach me your statutes!

The psalmist has made abundantly clear that he values the word of the Lord most highly, but in the opening words of this section he lays claim to the Lord himself. He wants to stress that God's word is not only given to his people to instruct them, but also, and indeed mainly, to invite them into fellowship with him. It is the chief means by which the Lord comes to his people and they draw near to him. Each has an inheritance in the other — he in them and they in him (Jer. 10:16; Deut. 32:9), a relationship that is more fully realized in the fact that Christians are joint-heirs of God with Jesus Christ (Rom. 8:17). It is glory begun below. God's word should never become a substitute for him. It will not be so in heaven.

My portion

The basic idea of the word 'portion' is 'a share'. It can refer to a person's daily food (Job 23:12), to a soldier's part of the plunder after victory (Gen. 14:24), or to a piece of ground that belongs to one's family (2 Kings 9:21, 25). All three uses are in the psalmist's mind because by the name 'LORD' he is recalling how God revealed himself at the time of the Exodus from Egypt. By that redemptive event he laid claim to his people according to the covenant that he had made with Abraham, Isaac and Jacob. They became his portion, his inheritance. He conquered their foes, fed them with manna, helped them dispossess the inhabitants of Canaan and gave them a place to live. His activity in these ways was highlighted by the fact that the Levites were provided for by him directly (Deut. 10:9).

The psalmist is showing that he understands all this and also the divine motivation of electing, self-giving love that lay behind it. In responsive love he is therefore choosing the Lord who has first chosen him (see 1 John 4:19). By the use of the singular possessive 'my', the psalmist is testifying to a personal appropriation of the covenant relationship, and by the word 'portion' he makes the Lord the one who provides his daily bread, and all that this implies, or the one who gives him resources, just as the wealth of the Egyptians was given to a company of fleeing slaves. But in the last line he uses a word which can mean 'land', and not only 'earth', and that leads one to think that this whole section is about living with the Lord in his land — and that means living in his love (v. 64). The psalmist is therefore not confining his thinking to what is terrestrial and physical but, like Abraham and all the people of faith, he is looking for the land that does flow with milk and honey, a city whose planner and builder is God (Heb. 11:10, 16). He is speaking about a foretaste of heaven.

The Christian is able to do more than merely echo the psalmist's words because the Lord has shown more of his love than the psalmist could anticipate. He has shown its stupendous nature by sending his own eternal Son (Rom. 5:8; 1 John 4:10) to bear the curse of a broken covenant for his people so that they might inherit heavenly blessings, begun below and consummated above. Every believer in Jesus should therefore be able to say 'my portion' and to do so with even more certainty and joy than the psalmist. Christians should know that they live 'in the Lord's love in his land' wherever they live in this fallen world, and also that every need will be met on the way to 'a new heavens and a new earth in which righteousness will dwell'. They have a heavenly Shepherd (Ps. 23) and they will never be either orphaned or exiled.

So how do they live 'here below'? The psalmist says three things about himself in this section. They are that he is a servant, a suppliant and a companion. We will consider each but they all interrelate.

A servant

The psalmist has already identified himself in this way (v. 49) and he will do so again (v. 65). In the first few verses of this section he declares that making the Lord one's portion involves submission and consecration to him. Trust in the Lord means self-renunciation (Prov. 3:5-6; Rom. 6:17). No one can obtain the blessings of salvation while retaining his own autonomy. Jesus is Lord as well as Saviour. The essence of being a servant is doing the will of God, and so the psalmist promises 'to keep' (vv. 57, 60, 63) his words. The word 'keep' is not only a synonym for 'obey', but also includes the idea of keeping safe, or guarding. The psalmist is determined to succeed where Adam failed, for the Lord's word is often distorted and falsified, and so his servants have real dangers to face.

There was opposition to be faced from the Israel of his day (v. 61; see also vv. 51, 53). 'Cords', or ropes, were used either for confining in one place or for dragging from one place to another. The wicked used such restrictive and oppressive practices against the psalmist, and that is just one aspect of the age-old opposition between those who belong to the serpent and those who are part of the 'seed of the woman' (see Gen. 3:15; Rev. 12). The psalmist sought to bring the Lord's land back under his authority so that it might be productive to his glory, and in that task he encounters resistance and threats. Still he refuses to put God's law out of his mind (v. 61).

This is often the case in the visible church. It was so for that true and special 'seed of the woman', the Lord Jesus Christ, who was 'the servant of the LORD' sent to turn back Israel to him so that the Gentiles might be gathered (Isa. 49:5-6). It has also been true of his followers, and it still is. There is no opposition like the opposition of the religious.

A suppliant

In the course of obeying the Lord the psalmist becomes aware of his own weakness.

He knows that his own 'ways' need to be scrutinized and corrected (v. 59). This is because they are the expression of his 'heart' (v. 58), whose inbuilt tendency is to wander because his thoughts and desires are not entirely under his control. This corresponds to what is often meant by the term 'flesh' in the New Testament, the constant plague of the Christian believer (2 Cor. 7:1; Gal. 5:16-17). To fail to keep a check on oneself and to assume that one is equal to any challenge or temptation is the high road to spiritual disaster, as was the case for Simon Peter (John 13:37-38; 1 Peter 5:6-11). Even if there were no 'world' and no 'devil', one's 'flesh' would be more than one could handle. A Christian believer can be his own worst enemy. There is ever a need to 'watch and pray' (see vv. 58-60; Mark 14:38), even if it can only be done at midnight (v. 62).

A companion

But he is aware that he is not alone in resisting the 'world' and 'the flesh' (and the devil) as he seeks to serve the Lord. There are others who 'fear' the Lord and the psalmist is glad to associate with them. Zion is where 'his friends and kindred dwell'. Together they talk in praise and prayer (see Ps. 122:6-9) and derive strength and comfort from each other's fellowship (see Mal. 3:16-18).

The church of Jesus Christ is also made up of servants, suppliants and companions, one's own folk (see Acts 4:23-37). They draw near to God, serve him and help each other onwards and upwards until the day dawns (Heb. 10:19-25) and the great international and innumerable multitude is gathered 'before the throne [of God] and before the Lamb' (see Rev. 7:9-10).

9.
THE GOOD, THE BAD AND THE BETTER

Psalm 119:65-72

⁶⁵ [Good you have done] with your servant,
    O LORD, according to your word.
⁶⁶ [Good judgement and knowledge teach me],
    for I believe in your commandments.
⁶⁷ Before I was afflicted I went astray,
    but now I keep your word.
⁶⁸ [Good you are and good you do];
    teach me your statutes.
⁶⁹ The insolent smear me with lies,
    but with my whole heart I keep your precepts;
⁷⁰ their heart is unfeeling like fat,
    but I delight in your law.
⁷¹ [Good it is] for me that I was afflicted,
    that I might learn your statutes.
⁷² [More good to me is the law of your mouth]
    than thousands of gold and silver pieces.

Goodness is the theme of this section of his poem and a few minor changes have been introduced into the ESV translation quoted above (see the phrases in square brackets) in order to make this clear. Five of its eight lines begin with the word 'good' and in one of them it is used twice (v. 68).¹

It is the goodness of the Lord, as revealed in his word and ways (vv. 65, 68), that the psalmist is celebrating. He knows full well that everything is not good in his own 'world' (vv. 67, 69-70), and so his exultation does not amount to escapism. He would not have shared Robert Browning's triumphalist view that 'God's in his heaven and all's right with the world.' He knows that the world is 'broken'; human beings are sinful. But he is no pessimist either, for he knows that God is good and does what is good. Truly, 'he [does] all things well'! (Mark 7:37).

The goodness of the Lord

'Goodness' is a term that has a wide range of uses in any language. In Hebrew it combines the ideas of what is morally right and what is aesthetically pleasant. All that God created was good (Gen. 1:31), and so were his arrangements for Adam and Eve in his garden — not only in what he provided, but even in what he prohibited. It was the devil's lie that broke the harmony between rectitude and appearance by depicting as advantageous what was in reality ruinous. As a result, 'all that glisters is not gold' in this fallen world. Human words and human deeds are not always expressive of goodness. But God is, and always will be, all good. All that he says and all that he does is good, even in this world that is marred and mangled by sin. What is more, he even makes the unpleasant to be beneficial! (v. 67). Behind his words and deeds are true and infinite 'judgement and knowledge'. He 'cannot lie' (Heb. 6:18) or 'do wickedness' (Job 34:10). Indeed, he is 'too wise to err, too good to be unkind'.

The bad

By means of his word as law and promise, the Lord set before Israel 'life and good', but also 'death and evil' (Deut. 30:15) if his way was not kept. He showed his people what was good (Micah 6:8), so that Israel possessed 'the embodiment of knowledge and truth' (Rom. 2:20). This was an immense privilege, but throughout the nation's history God's good word met with a mixed reception. In the psalmist's own day there were not only those who feared the Lord (v. 63), but also those who were 'wicked' (v. 61). As the apostle Paul wrote, 'They are not all Israel who are of Israel' (Rom. 9:6, NKJV).

Taking the psalmist as a representative of those who fear the Lord, it is clear that even they wander from the path (v. 67). But a line is drawn between them and the wicked, who are described as 'insolent'. This is a most important distinction. In the era when the Sinaitic covenant was valid, sins (apart from capital offences) were categorized according to whether they were sins of ignorance or sins committed with a 'high hand' (see Num. 15:1-36). The former were the result of human fallibility and were committed out of the frailty of either the mind or the affections. Sacrifices were provided for such cases, and the priest of the day was to receive such transgressors with compassion (see Heb. 5:1-2). But those who committed 'sins with a high hand' were deliberate covenant-breakers. With a 'hand [held] high' against the Lord, they rejected all his gracious provisions and operations in the covenant (see Heb. 6:4-6; 10:26-31). This was the reversal of the covenant oath. It was rebellion and high treason, and it could well have been true of at least some of the people whom the psalmist describes as rejecting the Lord's way and oppressing those who fear him (vv. 21, 51, 69, 78, 85, 122). He refers to the tongue and the 'heart' of such people (vv. 69, 70) in terms that paint a telling contrast

to the Lord's good word and ways — and even to those of
the psalmist himself.

Smearing the godly with lies

God always tells the truth and he requires his people to do
so too. The ninth commandment forbids 'false witness'
(Exod. 20:16), and fellowship with God in his house is denied
to those who slander (Ps. 15:3; 5:9; Rom. 3:13). Yet the insolent, like those who daub walls, set about vilifying the godly
in general conversation and perhaps also in legal proceed-
ings. Whether they had an actual hand in the psalmist's
affliction (v. 71) is not clear, but they could well have done,
and if that were so the effect would have been poverty, loss
of liberty, or injury, and not merely scorn. The differentiation between 'rich' and 'poor' in many Old Testament
passages (see Amos and Ezekiel) is to be understood in this
way, and in the New Testament too (James 5:1-6). Interestingly, riches are mentioned in verse 72.

Unfeeling like fat

God is concerned at man's plight and need. He is good to all
and his tender compassions are over all his works (Ps. 145:9).
But the insolent are equally impervious to any appeal from
him or to what they should have learned from a sense of
their own need. They should have derived spiritual benefit
from the testimony and conduct of the psalmist and his
companions (the true Israel), but they became disposed
against them. This obduracy of heart (see Isa. 6:10) has
echoes in the New Testament, both with regard to Jews
(John 12:40) and Gentiles (Eph. 4:17-18). When the truth is
suppressed God gives people over to the power of their own
ungodliness and unrighteousness (Rom. 1:18-32); when the
light that has been given is resisted, sight can be withdrawn
(2 Cor. 4:3-4). The Word of God exhibited in the walk of the ·

godly in the psalmist's day should have been 'a savour of life', but it became 'a savour of death' (2 Cor. 2:14-16, KJV).

All this was of course brought to a head in the life and ministry of Jesus. He sought out those who were neglected and despised by those who should have cared for them, incurring their scorn and slander, and he was killed for doing so (see Matt. 23). The 'insolent' of that day scorned the Good Shepherd and those whom he gathered. Unable to use his name and intending to defame him, they unwittingly spoke to his praise by saying, 'This man receives sinners and eats with them' (Luke 15:2).

The better

The psalmist has already confessed his love for God's commands (v. 48) and hope in his promises (v. 49). Now he turns back to them (v. 59) because he has wandered from the Lord (vv. 67, 71). In particular he wants to 'learn' them (v. 71) so that he no longer strays from them (v. 67), and to love them more than the most precious earthly things (v. 72). These are the thoughts and desires of a heart which God has kindly subdued and on which he has ineradicably inscribed his word by the Holy Spirit (see Ezek. 36:25-28; 2 Cor. 3:3). Old Testament saints shared the same sorrows and longings as new-covenant believers — and sometimes the latter can benefit from identifying with, and being instructed by, the former.

He first prays for a greater conformity to God's word, and he does so in terms which show that he has been truly enlightened. He asks 'the good LORD' to teach him 'judgement and knowledge' (v. 66) because he does believe in his commandments. He therefore wants to understand and apply what he believes. This means that he does not only want to be told what to do (or not do), but to be made truly wise. This is the exact opposite of Adam's weak-willed

submission to Satan's decision as to what would be good
and bad for him. The psalmist is therefore expressing trust
that God has good reasons for all he says and does. God is
neither whimsical nor arbitrary. He is good, and what he
says and does is good. And, what is more, he keeps his own
law! He does not determine something for man and then
claim the liberty of something different for himself. So the
psalmist asks to know how right God's commands are and
how wise his ways are, so that he might truly learn how to
live — and if that can only be thoroughly learned by affliction, then so be it. That is good as well (v. 71); it is only a
severe mercy.

Secondly, he professes the highest valuation of the Lord's
word, even though others despise it or prefer their own
'wisdom' or riches to it. 'Thousand' is the largest number in
Hebrew and here we have it in the plural! Gold and silver
were the currency of the day. It seems that the insolent were
the prosperous (and the powerful) in Israel and, as elsewhere, the righteous were the poor and the weak. But the
psalmist here is able to set all that aside — unlike David and
Asaph in Psalms 37 and 73 respectively. Riches are not evil,
but their real worth cannot be compared with the law of
God's mouth, which is more valuable. He will not exchange
the one for the other.

The insolent were a constant source of trouble to the
godly in Israel, as they were to the Lord himself and his
apostles. And this story does not end with them. In fact all
who say, 'The Lord is good and so are all his words and
ways,' will not be to the liking of those who are proud and
wilful. But while they do not think that their goodness can
compare with that of the Lord, they desire to be good like he
is — and one day they will be, and that for ever.

10.
A SPECTACLE FOR ALL

Psalm 119:73-80

[73] Your hands have made and fashioned me;
    give me understanding that I may learn your
      commandments.
[74] Those who fear you shall see me and rejoice,
    because I have hoped in your word.
[75] I know, O LORD, that your rules are righteous,
    and that in faithfulness you have afflicted me.
[76] Let your steadfast love comfort me
    according to your promise to your servant.
[77] Let your mercy come to me, that I may live;
    for your law is my delight.
[78] Let the insolent be put to shame,
    because they have wronged me with falsehood;
    as for me, I will meditate on your precepts.
[79] Let those who fear you turn to me,
    that they may know your testimonies.
[80] [Let] my heart be blameless in your statutes,
    that I may not be put to shame!

In this section the psalmist continues to think about both
the insolent and the reverent in Israel (vv. 74, 78, 79). His

main focus, however, is on himself, but that is only because he knows that he is to have an effect on both groups of people. Humbly, he appreciates his significance in a time of religious difficulty and affliction (vv. 73-75, 78). He has attracted the scorn and shame of the enemies of the Lord, and yet he knows that he is to encourage those who fear the Lord and put to shame those who do not. Like Paul and the apostles, he is 'a spectacle to the world, to angels, and to men' (see 1 Cor. 4:9).

All eyes are therefore upon him, and he knows it. But his own eyes are upon the Lord, and so in what follows (vv. 76-80) there are prayers for all concerned — for himself, for the wicked and for his friends. He is indeed a type of the Messiah and an example to all who follow in his steps, whether apostles or not (see 1 Cor. 4:9; Col. 1:24; 1 Peter 2:21-23). These verses cast a light on the story of the church militant, both in the New Testament and throughout subsequent history, even up to the present time.

His significance

The opening statement of this section is exceedingly rich in content. It should not be passed over as though it were merely an acknowledgement of his having been created by God — not that that could ever be something of minimal importance! Three things should be noted about it.

First, although the word translated 'made' is a common one in the Old Testament, as indeed it is in the English language, it is used in Genesis 1:26 in connection with man's uniqueness as 'the image of God'. It can therefore function as a variant for the word 'create', and that is so here.

Secondly, it is reinforced by the reference to God's 'hands', which is of course figurative, depicting God as a skilful workman giving personal attention to what he makes.

Thirdly, and most importantly, another verb is added, namely 'fashioned', a word that is used of setting up a throne or the founding of a city (Ps. 9:7; 107:36). By those terms and analogies this opening statement points to man as a creature of God, a ruler in God's world, under his authority and for his glory. It is a reference to man's constitution and the purpose of it.

The psalmist is therefore expressing a profound self-awareness. He knows that he is not only created by God, but that he has been given the capacity (and duty) to rule for God according to his word. As such he identifies himself as a servant of the Lord (v. 76). This supports the likelihood of his being a king in Israel. But, whether or not he is a king, he is resolved to enthrone God's word in the Israel of his day — and also in his own heart and life (see the second half of each of these lines). He is determined not to fall like Adam, and in that he is a conscious type of the Lord Jesus Christ, God's King over the church and the world (see Heb. 1:1-4).

His affliction

But there is something else that the psalmist says about himself, and he advertises it by using the expression, 'I know'. It is that he has been 'afflicted' (v. 75). He is therefore a suffering servant. This admission strikes a contrasting note to the emphasis he places on his created dignity in the first line (v. 73) and so it reflects on the fallen nature and circumstances of human life. This same pattern of thought is found in the inspired comment on Psalm 8 in Hebrews 2:5-9.

Of course the psalmist is not referring here either to Adam's fall, or to his own fall in Adam (Rom. 5:12), but what he is saying is traceable to the entry of sin into the world. The word for 'afflict' is used in the Old Testament to refer to bondage such as that of the Israelites in Egypt (Deut. 26:6-7) or to discipline because of sin committed (1 Kings 11:39).

Either of these senses (or both) would fit the after-effects of Adam's fall.

But the psalmist does not only admit that he has been brought low; he attributes this activity to the Lord and, what is more, he tells him so. Verse 75 is in the form of a direct address to God, and not a statement about him to others. Even so, it is neither a complaint nor a Job-like accusation but an acknowledgement of God's rectitude and of his care. 'Righteousness' is conformity to rule and here it is combined with 'faithfulness' — that is, consistency to promise. The psalmist is therefore submitting to God and trusting in him, believing that he has a good purpose in view by means of his affliction — whatever its cause. So did Jesus (see Heb. 5:8-10; John 17:1, 25), and so should Christian believers (1 Peter 3:17-22).

His supplications

Each of the lines in the latter part of this section begins with a verb whose mood is expressive of a polite command or urgent request. Translated 'let' or 'may', this verbal form is standard in the vocabulary of prayer. It was the tone of our Lord's praying in Gethsemane (see Matt. 26:39), but not of his high-priestly intercession (see John 17:1, 24).

The psalmist's prayers are therefore an expression of his desire that his lowly condition might not cloud the mani- festation of the glory of God to others. To that end he prays for himself (vv. 76, 77, 80), for the wicked (v. 78) and for those who fear the Lord (v. 79). Just as Jesus depended on communion with his own Father and the aid of the Holy Spirit in order to fulfil his Messianic ministry, so the psalm- ist makes his requests to God, desirous that his glory will be seen and appreciated.

For himself

Here the psalmist declares that he knows that he needs 'comfort' (v. 76; see also vv. 49-56), but comfort of the kind that enlivens and invigorates (v. 77). This is because, as God's servant, he has work to do for the Lord, over against the insolent but alongside those who want to know more of God's truth (vv. 78-79). The 'comfort' for which he prays comes from the Lord's 'steadfast love' and tender 'mercy', which is based on 'promise' (vv. 76-77). These terms are all covenant realities (see Exod. 34:5-7). He is therefore pleading the covenant relationship and asking for its blessings to be given to him. Even Jesus knew such assurances of his Father's love in the midst of his ministry (John 5:20; Luke 10:21) and so did the early Christians (see Acts 4:23-31). The Holy Spirit as 'Paraclete' supplies that need for companionship and courage (see John 14:18; 16:33).

What the psalmist asks for is something that is as real to him as the affliction he is enduring. It is not something notional but experiential, and to fail to take account of that will result in an approach to the psalms that lacks authenticity because the fully personal dimension is so prevalent in them.

For the insolent

The psalmist has already referred to the fact that he has been maligned unjustly (see v. 69) and has indicated that such vilification would not divert him from loyal obedience to God. Here he declares that he has had shame heaped on him falsely — whether in the public eye or in a court of law. When God's truth is set aside it is not long before justice succumbs to the same fate (vv. 85-86).

This unjust treatment could be part of the affliction referred to, or possibly the psalmist's affliction might have been regarded as a proof of God's displeasure with him, as was the case with Job, with Jesus himself (see Isa. 53:2-3) and with his disciples (see Matt. 5:11; Acts 6:12-14; 1 Peter 3: 14-17; 4:12-19). Those who ought to receive praise often find that they are regarded as worthy of blame (see Heb. 11:38). But the psalmist declares the goal he has set himself of being blameless by adhering inwardly and outwardly to God's law (vv. 78, 80).

As falsehood is made the basis for his condemnation, the psalmist prays that shame may be heaped on those who truly deserve it. This is a desire that sin will be judged and God will be honoured. It is a prayer for the vindication of God and of his people and is not vindictive.

For the faithful

Although the psalmist does not ignore the presence and malevolent activity of the wicked in this section, he refers more to those who fear the Lord. This is because they are of greater concern to him than his adversaries. He mentions them twice (vv. 74, 79). On the one hand he wants them to rejoice (v. 74) and, as a result of the way in which he perseveres in spite of his affliction (v.79), to learn more of the Lord's testimonies, whether promises or precepts. He is intent on gathering them together and providing them with encouragement. The prophet Isaiah did this in his day (Isa. 26:20) and it also happened in the time of Malachi (Mal. 3:16-18). The ministry of the Lord Jesus to his disciples in the upper room (John 13 – 17) is the classic example of this, and also the testimony of the apostle Paul as he wrote to the church at Philippi (Phil. 1: 19 – 2:30).

11.
THE SENTENCE OF DEATH

Psalm 119:81-88

⁸¹ My soul longs for your salvation;
  I hope in your word.
⁸² My eyes long for your promise;
  I ask, 'When will you comfort me?'
⁸³ For I have become like a wineskin in the smoke,
  yet I have not forgotten your statutes.
⁸⁴ How long must your servant endure?
  When will you judge those who persecute me?
⁸⁵ The insolent have dug pitfalls for me;
  they do not live according to your law.
⁸⁶ All your commandments are sure;
  they persecute me with falsehood; help me!
⁸⁷ They have almost made an end of me on earth,
  but I have not forsaken your precepts.
⁸⁸ In your steadfast love give me life,
  that I may keep the testimonies of your mouth.

What the psalmist says in this section shows that he believes himself to be in desperate straits. He sounds a new note in his address to God. In addition to making a specific request of the kind that he has made before (v. 88; see v. 25), he now

takes God to task. He gives voice to three rhetorical questions (vv. 82, 84) and underlines them by the specific expression 'I ask' (v. 82) and also by an exclamatory prayer:
'Help me!' (v. 86). Such urgency must not be overlooked and
the reason or explanation for it has to be sought.

A wineskin in the smoke

This simile provides a way in to the psalmist's mind at this
time. Although it is not among the figurative expressions
from the Bible (usually from the King James Version) that
have found their way into spoken English — for example,
'the skin of one's teeth' (Job 19:20) and 'the eye of the needle'
(Matt. 19:24) — it is not difficult to get the impression that
the idea it conveys is not a positive or pleasant one. 'A
wineskin in the smoke' belongs to another culture from our
own, but it sounds ominous, a bit like 'salt that has lost its
savour'.

But what is the precise point of the simile? Wineskins
were in effect leather bottles that contained water (Gen.
21:14, 19), milk (Judg. 4:19) or wine (1 Sam. 16:20). They were
made from whole skins of animals with the holes sewn up
where heads and limbs had been cut off. They were hung on
camels as people journeyed, or on a tent wall when they
were at rest, and in a desert climate these containers were
liable to degrade in a fairly short time. There was one occasion in Israel's history when 'worn-out and torn and
mended' wineskins and food sacks were used to support a
lie and Israel's leaders were deceived (see Josh. 9). Hung on
the wall of a tent, they would quickly become blackened
from the smoke of a fire and likely to split through becoming shrivelled up. That is the kind of thing the psalmist
seems to have had in mind — the end of his life's usefulness
in some way or other.

'The end'

The psalmist describes himself therefore as being in some extremity and he brings this out by a verb that contains within itself the idea of 'an end'. He does so three times in these eight lines and in important places in the section. He employs the word in each of the opening two lines and also in the last-but-one line. Unfortunately (in my opinion) the ESV translation obscures this fact by opting for the rendering 'long for' in the first two lines and 'make an end' in the penultimate line. It would have been better if the word 'fail' had been used because that is more indicative of an end.

The verb is a key term for the whole section and some things should be noted about the ways in which it is used.

First, and depending on its grammatical form, the verb can either mean 'to come to an end' or 'to be brought to an end' and the psalmist uses it in both ways. In verses 81 and 82 he is referring to himself as in some sense 'coming to an end'; in verse 87 he sees himself as in some way being 'brought to an end' by the actions of others. The condition that the psalmist describes is therefore a double-sided one.

Secondly, and depending on its context, it can be used in a metaphorical or a literal sense, and both of those are also found in this section because the psalmist describes his situation in both psychological and physical terms.

The word that begins each of the first two lines is repeated for the sake of emphasis. It records the psalmist's complete lack of inner resources in the face of his great need. He is overcome with a kind of feebleness. Sometimes it is translated by the word 'fail', and that is preferable for the reason given above. 'To long for' is inadequate to convey the meaning. Something more like 'consumed with longing' (v. 20) is what is called for, although a different Hebrew word is used at that place. In these opening verses the verb is used metaphorically, but when it reappears towards the end of the section (v. 87) it has a literal or physical sense.

There the psalmist speaks of the likelihood of his being removed from the face of the earth. His prayer for 'life' (v. 88) therefore covers the need of body as well as spirit. 'Soul' in verse 81 is not the spiritual part of a human being, but the whole person.

This 'near-death' experience that the psalmist describes is, however, not only the result of the activities of his foes, but more particularly of the non-intervention of the Lord in answer to his prayers (vv. 84, 85). From a survey of previous verses it can be seen that their opposition has been mounting (see vv. 42, 51, 69, 78) and that it now reaches some kind of critical point. Interestingly, the word used here for 'smoke' is found in only one other place in the Old Testament. This is in Genesis 19:28, where it describes the destruction of Sodom and Gomorrah and the scene is specifically compared to 'the smoke of a furnace'. The psalmist is confronting a desperate situation which calls for God to intervene in salvation (v. 81) and judgement (v. 84), as he did at the Exodus. But the Lord has not done so! The psalmist has been asking for 'comfort' and for justice — that is, for covenant blessings — but these have not been forthcoming in spite of the word of promise (vv. 81-82). Now he asks again three times when that will happen, or how long it will be before it does (vv. 82, 84), and he also requests immediate assistance (vv. 82, 84, 86). The Lord Jesus Christ prayed three times in his hour of great need when his soul was 'exceedingly sorrowful, even to death' in the Garden of Gethsemane (see Matt. 26:37-46, NKJV; Mark 14:32-42). So did the apostle Paul in connection with his thorn in the flesh (2 Cor. 12:8).

But not the end

It is divine inactivity or silence in the face of extreme hostility that has caused the psalmist his most acute anguish, just as it was with the Saviour (see Ps. 22:1-2; Matt. 27:46). But, like the Messiah whom he typifies, the psalmist neither gives in to the wicked nor gives up in his devotion to the Lord. The anticipated end does not come, as is evident from the fact that that there is as much of the psalm still to come as has been composed so far, but also because the last line of this section (the halfway point of the poem) makes clear that the Lord has been answering his prayers and upholding him albeit without his knowing it. So, 'the end' that he fears is not actually the end. Instead, it is only another conscious 'beginning' in the grace of God.

The last line of this section contains three things to note. They stand in striking contrast to all the difficulties previously recorded. The first is that once again the psalmist confesses that the Lord's love is steadfast (see earlier comments and also Psalm 136, where such a declaration follows each instance given of the Lord's dealings with Israel). Secondly, he still believes that the Lord can and will meet his great need for 'life', and so 'death' will not prevail. Thirdly, it is his intention to carry on as he has been living, maintaining the words of the Lord even though he is surrounded by those who do not keep God's law.

The psalmist's words in this very section show that while his fears were real, they were in fact groundless (see Ps. 73:1). The old wineskin did not then crack (see Mark 2:22), but the day would come when the richer wine of the new covenant (see John 2:1-10) would require a new wineskin (see Heb. 8:7-13). Living in the midst of dying is, however, the hallmark of true believers in both dispensations of the covenant of grace (see Heb. 11:13-22), but the death and resurrection of the Lord Jesus make an immense difference to those who suffer in his cause and service (see 2 Cor. 1:8-11; 4:7-12).

12.
LONG AND WIDE

Psalm 119:89-96

[89] For ever, O LORD, your word
   is firmly fixed in the heavens.
[90] Your faithfulness endures to all generations;
   you have established the earth, and it stands fast.
[91] By your appointment they stand this day,
   for all things are your servants.
[92] If your law had not been my delight,
   I would have perished in my affliction.
[93] I will never forget your precepts,
   for by them you have given me life.
[94] I am yours; save me,
   for I have sought your precepts.
[95] The wicked lie in wait to destroy me,
   but I consider your testimonies.
[96] I have seen a limit to all perfection,
   but your commandment is exceedingly broad.

The opening word of this section introduces a surprising note because the psalmist has just been contemplating 'the end'. He was filled with alarm because his physical safety was threatened and his spiritual strength was depleted (see discussion in the previous chapter). He still remembers that 'affliction' (v. 92) and, what is more, the danger from the wicked still exists, so that it cannot be ignored (vv. 94, 95). But his prayers for 'life' have been answered (vv. 92, 93) and he has been given a greater understanding and appreciation of the Lord and his word in relation to the world in which he finds himself. As a consequence, he can use the expression 'for ever', and he does so twice. The first of these relates to the Lord (v. 89) and the second, which is not so obvious in translation, relates to himself. 'I will never' (v. 93) is really, 'For ever I will not'. Such certainty is also the theme of the following sections.

At the core of the Hebrew term translated 'for ever' is a word that relates to time in its length. From the standpoint of a speaker or writer it can refer either to the past (see Ps. 77:5) or to the future (Neh. 2:3). Stretching backwards and forwards, it is always used in an indeterminate sense, unlike 'this day' (v. 91). It can therefore refer not only to antiquity or to futurity, but even to eternity. It is used of the Lord himself, who is 'the Everlasting [i.e. for ever] God' (see Gen. 21:33) and also of his truth ('faithfulness' in v. 90) and mercy ('steadfast love' in v. 88), which are combined in Psalm 117. Taking into account the ongoing course of biblical revelation, the term 'for ever' flows into the word 'eternal' which is so prevalent in John's Gospel, where, referring to something that is 'heavenly', it necessarily contains the idea of that which is everlasting.

The word of the Lord

'Word' and 'deed' are expressed by the same noun in Hebrew. This is a consequence of the fact that what God says he does (see Gen. 1:3, 5; Luke 1:37). This is so with regard to both the creation of the world and the redemption of his people (see Ps. 33:4-9). Obviously it is the created

universe that the psalmist is thinking of in these opening
lines as he specifies 'the heavens' and 'the earth'. But his
emphasis is not so much on the creative power of the word
of God as on the continuance of all that has been created.
He does not use the verb 'create' or 'make', but 'fix', 'estab-
lish' and 'stand' (vv. 89-91). 'And it was so' therefore figures
more prominently in his mind at this point than 'Let there
be ...' (Gen. 1:6, 7).

The word of the Lord does not only bring into being what
is in 'the heavens above, the earth beneath and the waters
under the earth', but it also makes them what they are and
keeps them so from one generation to another. All this is in
accordance with his 'appointment' (ESV), or 'judgements'. It
is God's authoritative decrees that comprise natural law. The
psalmist therefore highlights divine government as well as
production. The one who brings things animate and inani-
mate into being by his word also appoints them their
spheres and functions. They are neither self-originating nor
self-determining. They are his 'servants', and as such they do
his bidding (v. 91; cf. Ps. 147:15, 18).

This orderliness that is evident in such a variety of things
and processes exists only as a result of the stability inherent
in the everlasting Lord which he puts into effect by means of
his word. The world does not run itself. The New Testament
speaks of Christ the Word as not only creating all things, but
maintaining them and keeping them together in spite of the
disharmony and divisiveness introduced by sin: 'All things
were created through him and for him. And he is before all
things, and in him all things hold together' (Col. 1:16-17).

The 'for ever' of the godly

This use of the term 'for ever' is also positive in meaning
although it is couched in a negative expression. It is reminiscent of the line of the hymn, 'never, no never, no never',

which is based on Hebrews 13:5 — a verse that contains repeated negations. The psalmist's contemplation of the stability of the natural world that is the result of the Lord's dynamic word has put such strength into his soul that, if everything that the Lord has brought into being stands and serves him, then so will he. The psalmist is therefore expressing a strong determination in this way — and one that is as long as it is strong! By means of it he is rejecting the possibility of any time limit being put on his devotion to the Lord and his word in the world.

He expresses his devotion in several ways in the second part of this section.

First, he will never forget God's precepts. They have been the means by which the Lord has given him fresh life (v. 93). The noun 'precept' refers specifically to oversight and administration. The realization that the Lord does have everything under his control and direction brings him comfort and strength. God does work all things together for good to those who love him (Rom. 8:28).

Secondly, he consecrates himself afresh to the Lord in prayer. By saying, 'I am yours; save me,' he reminds the Lord of his covenant responsibility to save him time and time again in every evil circumstance (v. 94). God's saving power is more than enough to 'deliver [him] from every evil work and preserve [him] unto his heavenly kingdom' (2 Tim. 4:18, KJV). He counts on it.

Thirdly, he will consult God's word most closely in spite of the fact that the wicked seek to entrap him (v. 95). His concern will be to walk in obedience to God's word and to leave to the Lord all the consequences of doing so.

The closing line of this section contains a surprise in each of its parts.

'The end of all perfection'

First, the psalmist reintroduces the idea of an 'end' into that expanse of endlessness that he has been contemplating both for the word and for himself in relation to it. He speaks explicitly about the 'end of all perfection' (v. 96, literal translation). What does that mean? The word that is translated 'perfection' is used frequently in the previous section in other forms but appears nowhere else in the Old Testament. It could be rendered by the word 'end', as in verse 87. 'Completeness' and 'perfection' are the possible translations of the noun here. Both are ends of sorts and the latter term is usually opted for.

The 'broad' commandment

Secondly, he uses the adjective 'broad', changing the standard of measurement that he has been using for the word and for himself. He is no longer looking backwards and forwards, but from side to side. Why does he do that?

The expression 'I have seen' is important and useful in answering these questions. It is reminiscent of Ecclesiastes, where it is a frequent refrain. There Solomon 'sees' (in other words, he surveys and analyses) 'life under the sun' — that is, life in a fallen world. He looks in all directions, taking in natural things and processes and also human pursuits and achievements, before coming to 'the end of the matter', the last word, which is also the first one, namely to 'fear God and keep his commandments' (Eccles. 12:13).

The psalmist here does something similar. He casts his mental net far and wide and 'sees' that in a designed and governed world everything has its place and purpose, much of it great and good, but not all. However, it all has its 'end' — whether that is understood as its termination in the judgement (the word for 'end' in verse 96 can be used in that sense — see Gen. 6:13), or to its inclusion in the consummation of the kingdom of God. But what will never be the case will be that the Word of God will be cut down to size, shown to be small or unimportant by anything that claims to be bigger and better. It is 'exceedingly broad'. It brings to an end all that opposes it, but gives a place in its greater and grander scheme of things (the kingdom of God) to the greatest ideas, remedies and reforms, discoveries and achievements. The new heavens and earth are produced by the word of God every bit as much as the old creation, and it is because of Christ's blood that there will be a new world and new inhabitants (Col. 1:15-23). And Jesus Christ, the incarnate Word, will have the pre-eminence that is his due!

13.
TAUGHT BY GOD

Psalm 119:97-104

[97] Oh how I love your law!
      It is my meditation all the day.
[98] Your commandment makes me wiser than my enemies,
      for it is ever with me.
[99] I have more understanding than all my teachers,
      for your testimonies are my meditation.
[100] I understand more than the aged,
      for I keep your precepts.
[101] I hold back my feet from every evil way,
      in order to keep your word.
[102] I do not turn aside from your rules,
      for you [yourself] have taught me.
[103] How sweet are your words to my taste,
      sweeter than honey to my mouth!
[104] Through your precepts I get understanding;
      therefore I hate every false way.

At the close of the previous section the psalmist sounded like Solomon in the book of Ecclesiastes, and in these verses there is much that is reminiscent of the book of Proverbs. True wisdom is what is in the psalmist's mind at this point in his poem. He refers to it as being conveyed by means of God's word and expressed in a life that is distinctive in both its inward and outward aspects. He claims to possess (more of) it in contrast to others (vv. 98-100), but only because he has been taught by God (v. 102; see also John 6:45).

The Teacher

Like many other Bible versions, the ESV translation of verse 102 renders the Hebrew as 'You have taught me'. This is not inaccurate, but it is inadequate. The rendering should be 'You yourself have taught me' (see NASB and NIV) because the psalmist uses the pronoun 'you' twice in the latter half of this line, once as part of the verb 'have taught', but also separately from the verb. This doubling feature is not an example of verbal redundancy. (Is there such a thing as 'padding' in Scripture?) It is a way of expressing emphasis.

The psalmist's stress on divine teaching should be given due attention. It expresses the important truth that God makes use of his recorded word in order to achieve the purpose for which he gave and intended it (see 2 Tim. 3:14-17). Just as he does not leave the created universe to run by its own inherent power, but upholds it moment by moment, as we saw in the previous section, so the word of God does not become effective simply because it has acquired textual form. God speaks with his own voice through what he caused to be infallibly written in human language, and as a result it becomes 'profitable'.

Care must therefore be taken not to emphasize the written Word and the character and conduct that it requires to the neglect of the only agency by which that truth becomes actual and operative in a person's life. The psalmist does not do this. He has the perfect combination here of the law and the Lord which, put in Christian terms, is equivalent to the Word and Spirit. Neither one replaces the other.

They are neither to be identified nor separated, but they are to be distinguished. The Word of God is merely an instrument; the Spirit of God is the living agent.

The explanation of God's 'success' as a teacher does not only lie in his totally comprehensive knowledge, but in that power which gives him access to the human heart (i.e. mind) and exerts a subduing and illuminating influence over it. No one teaches like him (see Job 36:22; Ps. 25:8-10). For the first time the psalmist says that he loves God's law (v. 97; see also vv. 113, 127) and, speaking of the commandments as if they were all rolled into one, he says, '*It* is [for] ever with me' (v. 98). In this further use of the term 'for ever' (see the previous chapter) the idea of permanence is combined with presence. 'With me' is really 'to me', or 'of me' — that is, 'mine'. The Lord's word is not merely 'with' him as an accompaniment; it is his possession. We may say that it was so much a part of him that it was within him. (Like Bunyan his blood was, to quote Spurgeon, 'bibline' too!). The law was 'written on [his] heart' (Ps. 40:8; 2 Cor. 3:3).

The psalmist was therefore a true Israelite (Rom. 2:28-29). He had been born again, and that is what differentiated him from the groups to which he makes reference in these verses, as we shall see. Old Testament saints were regenerated no less than New Testament ones. The difference between them lay in an understanding and appreciation of that inward work (cf. John 15:3) which could only be obtained after, and because of, Christ's exaltation and the gift of the Holy Spirit.

The untaught

The psalmist refers to three groups of people — his enemies, his teachers and the aged. None of these possessed the wisdom that he had been given, even though they all belonged to the Israel of his day.

His enemies

His 'enemies' have often been referred to in previous sections — most recently as 'the wicked' (v. 95). They were not
without some knowledge of God's revealed and recorded
law, because they are described as 'forsaking' it (see vv.
53, 85), and doing so arrogantly (vv. 21, 51, 69, 78, 85). But
they had no understanding of it. This is another example of
the age-old conflict between the seed of the woman and that
of the serpent. They are the psalmist's enemies only because
he is a friend of God, of his law and of those who fear the
Lord. They do not think of God, let alone of his law (Ps. 14;
53; see Rom. 3:9-18).

His teachers

His 'teachers' are mentioned here for the first and last time.
We have little to go on with regard to their identity except
that are not the same group as 'the aged' and of course are
not among the 'enemies'. Earlier he has referred to himself
as a 'young man' and to the importance of being taught so
that future leaders might be provided for the people of God.
Such teaching was first of all the task of the father (Deut.
6:4-9, 20-25), but it was connected with the responsibility
assigned to both parents (see Gen. 1:26; Exod. 20:12).

The aged

The 'aged' were the 'fathers' of the tribe or society and were
to be greatly respected (see Job 32:6-7). The implication is
that both of these groups were not devoid of wisdom, but it
was a wisdom that did not result in the meditation (v. 99)
that led to obedience (v. 100).

The Lord Jesus was surrounded by such people too, the
unteachable and those with less knowledge than he had. At
twelve years of age he was able both to answer hard questions

and to ask even harder ones of the religious leaders of his
day, whether friendly or not. In addition he knew more
about himself and the reason for his existence on earth than
even his earthly parents did (Luke 2:40-52). Later in his life,
when almost all the leaders were opposed to him, they could
not defeat him with regard to knowledge of the Scriptures
(Matt. 22). He had even more understanding than the
psalmist possessed!

The taught

The features of having been taught by God are also presented in these verses and, although the psalmist only refers
to himself here, we may safely assume that the same was
true of all who feared the Lord (see vv. 63, 79). Earlier we
noted that he refers to both the inward and outward effects
of such teaching, and that is so here.

The inward effects

Inwardly, he speaks of the activity of the mind and the
emotions with regard to God's word. Together they are
aspects of the 'love' of which he speaks and they are not to
be set in opposition to each other. If either is regarded as
the enemy of the other the result is something theoretical or
sentimental. He refers not only to the mind, but also to the
mouth and (speaking metaphorically) expresses what he
thinks about God's word in terms of tasting it (v. 103). The
result is delight as well as insight. There are spiritual senses.
Paul talks about 'the eyes' of the 'heart' or 'mind' (see Eph.
1:18).

The outward effects

Outwardly, the psalmist's conduct is powerfully affected.
The uniting of understanding and affection directs and

propels the 'feet' away from what is 'evil [and] false' and towards what is in keeping with God's own 'testimonies' (v. 99), which are good and true.

Sin disrupts as well as corrupts. It causes disturbance between man and God and between man and man — and also within a human being. It sets desires against thoughts and dragoons the will against any better judgement. Regeneration reintegrates mind, heart and will and reorientates a person to the Lord, his word and ways. It makes a sinner whole again, and that is shown here in what the psalmist says.

14.
WORDS ABOUT THE WORD

Psalm 119:105-112

[105] Your word is a lamp to my feet
and a light to my path.
[106] I have sworn an oath and confirmed it,
to keep your righteous rules.
[107] I am severely afflicted;
give me life, O LORD, according to your word!
[108] Accept [the freewill offerings of my mouth], O LORD,
and teach me your rules.
[109] I hold my life in my hand continually,
but I do not forget your law.
[110] The wicked have laid a snare for me,
but I do not stray from your precepts.
[111] Your testimonies are my heritage for ever,
for they are the joy of my heart.
[112] I incline my heart to perform your statutes
for ever, to the end.

The opening line of this section is probably the best-known verse in the whole psalm. It can be regarded as presenting the main theme of the poem, and doing so in terms which are also easily understood in every culture. What is more, it

can be considered as a confession of biblical faith, whether
that of an Old Testament or New Testament saint, and even
of the Lord Jesus Christ himself in his life of obedience on
earth. It contains, among others, the following seminal
truths: firstly, that the world is in a realm of darkness;
secondly, that the word comes from a realm of light; and,
thirdly, that it enlightens all who receive it and leads them
to the realm of light from which it came. It gathers so many
biblical passages around itself.

This incredibly rich statement must, however, be exam-
ined in its own setting, and in order to do so we shall focus
on two expressions, namely 'light' (v. 105) and 'freewill
offerings' (v. 108). The content of the other lines of the
section will be considered in connection with these points.
The term 'for ever' that appeared in verses 89-96 is also
found here (vv. 111, 112).

Light

The word 'light' occurs in only one other place in this psalm
(see v. 130), and there it recalls the government of the
universe and the guidance of the people of God in the
wilderness. On the fourth day of creation the sun, moon and
stars were set in place to 'give light upon the earth' (see Gen.
1:14-19), and for forty years in the wilderness a pillar of fire
gave 'light' by night (Ps. 78:14). The psalmist has just referred to the fact that he has more wisdom than others, and
in verse 130 he points out the way in which that happens.
Just as an opened door discloses what lies behind it, so the
word that is 'opened' by its Author discloses his 'wonders'
(see vv. 18, 129). The Lord enlightens those whom he teaches
(see 1 Cor. 2:6-16).

The existence of 'darkness' is of course presupposed by
what is said here, but that word is nowhere used in the poem.
It is, however, necessarily implied in what the psalmist says

about meditating at night-time (vv. 55, 62, 147, 148).
Whether that was something forced on him by adverse
circumstances (v. 107) or whether it was a matter of choice
on his part is not clear, but physical darkness is necessarily
presupposed by what he says in those verses. However, in
addition he also refers to a darkness that is to be seen in the
daytime by referring to those who reject the Lord and his
law and who hunt his people (v. 110). That darkness shrouds
the mind and heart and rules the mouth and the feet. It is
the exact opposite of what is said about wisdom in the
previous section.

The psalmist has just referred to his 'feet' (v. 101) and it
might seem as though he does the same again here. But
there is a slight difference between the two nouns which is
surprising but significant. In verse 105 the Hebrew does not
have 'my feet' but 'my foot'. He is therefore referring to
every step that he takes on a path (lamp in hand) in accord
with his solemn and subsequently confirmed vow to keep
the Lord's precepts (v. 106). He is on a pilgrim path through
a dark world and every step on the way is to be directed by
obedience to God's law.

So it is with the Christian believer, whose freedom from
the moral law only relates to its condemning curse and not
to its righteous precepts (see John 8:12; 9:40-41; 12:35-36;
1 John 1:5 – 2:11; Rom. 13:8-14; Eph. 4:18-19; 5:8-14; 2 Peter
1:16-21). Bondage to sin and death is replaced by a delight
and a duty to keep the law, not by a permit to dismiss it (see
Gal. 5:13-26). The gospel of Christ leads to the law of Christ
(Gal. 6:2; Matt. 5:17-48; 11:28-30).

Freewill offerings

One of the 'omissions' from this poem is any clear reference
to the corporate worship of Israel and its sacrificial features,
but the mention here of 'freewill offerings' shows that the

piety which the psalmist is expressing was not contrary to the provisions of the Sinaitic legislation. 'Freewill offerings' were those that were voluntarily made in addition to those stipulated for special feasts (Lev. 22:18; Deut. 12:6). They expressed confession of sin, gratitude for mercy or answers to prayer, and consecration to the Lord's service (see Lev. 1 – 7).

But what can 'freewill offerings of *the mouth*' refer to? (See the altered translation of verse 108 at the head of the chapter.) While it is possible that reference is being made to the fulfilment of a previously made vow (v. 106), there is another interesting possibility. 'Freewill offerings' were made in connection with the construction of the tabernacle and temples, but these were not animal sacrifices. They were sacrificial gifts of materials and minerals, animal skins, precious stones and costly spices (see Exod. 35:29; 36:3; 2 Chr. 31:14; Ezra 1:4). But how are these connected with 'the mouth'? By way of a metaphor for words — and these are not only words of 'praise', as echoed in Hebrews 13:15. Words of prayer (see Hosea 14:2) are also to be included — see the plea, 'Accept ...', at the beginning of the verse, which is a plea for gracious reception and effective use. And that being so, why should not preaching be included as well, because that is what the psalmist is in effect doing in this psalm? Psalm 19:14 has a similar petition:

> Let the words of my mouth and the meditation of my
>   heart [i.e. mind]
>   be acceptable in your sight,
>   O LORD, my rock and my redeemer.

Just as 'freewill offerings' built the Lord's house materially in Old Testament times, so words about the word, and in keeping with it, build it spiritually (see Isa. 66:1-2). In the new-covenant era this is equally true, but it is more evident and glorious, for the gospel word founds and builds, governs and guides the church (see Acts 19:8-10, 20; Eph. 2:20-22;

4:11-16, 25-32; 5:19-20; 6:18; cf. by way of contrast, Eph. 5:12). It does so through the ministry of the word in preaching, prayer, praise and mutual edification. Nothing is to replace Holy Scripture in the life of the church. The Holy Spirit will always bless it.

As has been noted, the psalmist prays that the Lord will 'accept' his words about the word — that is, that he will do so graciously. The word that is translated 'accept' is often used in connection with blood sacrifice. God can only be gracious through the atoning death of the Lord Jesus Christ, and even his believing people cannot depend on any supposed 'merit' of their service to him. But he will hear and answer a plea for his grace; that is what the psalmist expresses in the rest of this section. He reminds the Lord that his words have arisen out of a mind that has been consecrated to keep his word (v. 106), a spirit that needs to be sustained in a time of great adversity and frailty (vv. 107, 109-110) and an intention to make God's word his habitat (v. 111), just as each of the tribes was allocated a portion of the promised land as its own to be subdivided among its constituent families. The word of the Lord conveys the blessings of the heavenly Canaan — 'a good and a broad land' (Exod. 3:8) and a 'goodly heritage' (Ps. 16:6, KJV) — to every Christian believer. And not only did the Lord accept the psalmist's words, but he is still using them today for the good of his pilgrim people!

15.
SUPPORT IN TRIALS

Psalm 119:113-120

[113] I hate the double-minded,
   but I love your law.
[114] You are my hiding place and my shield;
   I hope in your word.
[115] Depart from me, you evildoers,
   that I may keep the commandments of my God.
[116] Uphold me according to your promise, that I may live,
   and let me not be put to shame in my hope!
[117] Hold me up, that I may be safe
   and have regard for your statutes continually!
[118] You spurn all who go astray from your statutes,
   for their cunning is in vain.
[119] All the wicked of the earth you discard like dross,
   therefore I love your testimonies.
[120] My flesh trembles for fear of you,
   and I am afraid of your judgements.

The name of the consonant which was to begin the lines of
this section evidently suggested a theme to the psalmist that
chimed in with his circumstances. There is a Hebrew verb
'samakh' which means 'to lean on' (see Judg. 16:26). Used

metaphorically, it expresses both dependence (see Prov. 3:5) and maintenance (see Ps. 37:17, 24), for 'the LORD upholds' those who trust in him. That verb appears here in verse 116 with a synonym being used in the following line (see also Ps. 18:35).

The psalmist was well aware that he needed divine support because in every line of this section he refers to the wicked in one way or another. They are in the background in verses 114 and 117, but to the fore in every other line, and in verse 115 he describes them as 'evildoers' for the first time. Clearly the psalmist is experiencing a time of trial, and it is of some severity, because it leads him to anticipate the coming judgement of God (v. 120).

The current trial

As has been mentioned earlier, the word for 'judgements' often means 'judicial rulings'. A judge gives a verdict on a case before him as to who is in the right and who is in the wrong. The psalmist is surrounded by the 'wicked of the land' (the word translated 'earth' in the ESV can also mean 'land', see v. 64), whom he describes in a number of ways — for example, they wander (deliberately) from God's statutes and they are deceitful (v. 118). He has spoken of them in this way before (see vv. 85, 86). But he also says some new things about them. They are 'double-minded' (v. 113) — and that does not mean that they have moments of doubt! It means that they are like two different persons in one body; they could be said to have a 'double heart' (see, by way of contrast, Num. 14:24; 1 Chr. 12:33; cf. Hosea 10:2; 1 Kings 11:6; 18:21). This is the ultimate in deceit (v. 118), which is hypocrisy. The psalmist is therefore surrounded by Israelites who reject God's reign although they claim to serve him. In reality they are those who do, or practise, 'evil', and the psalmist calls this by its shocking name (v. 115) and will have no truck with it (v. 101). 'Evil' denotes not only the absence of all that is truly good, but the presence of the opposite.

These circumstances in which the psalmist finds himself resemble those at Sinai and later at Baal Peor (see Exod. 32; Num. 25). What he does is to take the Lord's side (see Exod. 32:26) in this covenant dispute with his people, as did the tribe of Levi and Phinehas respectively on those occasions. The same principle may be seen at work in connection with Caleb and Joshua and their report of the land over against the rest of the spies and the unbelieving people (see Num. 13 – 14). The psalmist draws a line between himself and those who do not keep God's commandments (v. 115). He loves God and his law (vv. 113, 119); they, by implication, do not. He shuns them so that he may be faithful to 'his' God.

This conflict came to a climax in our Lord's earthly life (see Matt. 23:13-36), but it continues in the lives of his servants (see John 16:1-4). All the events in the wilderness already referred to are recalled and envisaged in the New Testament (see 1 Cor. 10; Heb. 4; Jude; Rev. 2 – 3). Eternal destiny may be suspended on that moment of time when a decisive fidelity to 'the faith once delivered to the saints' is called for in the church.

The psalmist therefore lived in an 'evil day' (see Eph. 6:13). How did he react? It is one thing to resolve to 'leave the world's side and face the foe', but how can that actually be done? The psalmist knew the answer to that question. He had a God to turn to (v. 115) who would uphold him (v. 116). Confident supplication and dependence therefore character-ize the communion recorded in these verses, and they are fed by two convictions.

First, he knows that God is his 'hiding place', or 'refuge', and a 'shield'. He uses the pronoun 'my' before each of those nouns (v. 114), which together point to complete protection — that is, concealment and defence (see also Ps. 91:1-4).

Secondly, the psalmist knows that God rejects those who reject him (vv. 118, 119) as 'dross' (i.e. base metal separated from the pure by the refining process). Psalm 1:4 uses a winnowing analogy for the same truth and refers to chaff that the wind blows away. There is no good use for dross or chaff, but the righteous are precious in the sight of the Lord (see Mal. 3:17-18). The psalmist therefore asks God for strength to continue to hope in him and obey his word, and also for safety as he does so (vv. 116, 117).

Similarly, Christians know that 'their' God is both good and just and that he will provide for those who persevere. They can address the psalmist's God as their God and Father through Jesus Christ and ask for strength to glorify him in their own 'evil day' (see Eph. 6:13; Phil. 1:19-21; 2 Tim. 4:18).

The coming trial

The psalmist has drawn a line between himself and the wicked in the Israel of his day. He has made a judgement as to what his duty is in terms of his being in covenant with the Lord. But he is also aware that God will draw a line when he makes his judgements known in the land (vv. 118-121), and that is something that causes him great apprehension. In verse 120 he uses three terms to describe it that combine the psychological and the physical elements of the human constitution, the latter being the effect of the former. He speaks of his 'flesh' bristling and twice refers to his fear of God.

Before anyone comes to the conclusion that this is a response that is less than what gospel grace should effect, and that it therefore has nothing to say to a Christian, it ought to be noted that the psalmist also speaks of 'love' as he contemplates this solemn intervention of God to sift his visible church. He knows that the remnant will be preserved in that judgement (see Amos 9:9). But he is also aware that he must pass through it, just as others did at the Flood, the Red Sea and the Jordan, at the fall of Samaria and Jerusalem and in the consequent exile, and it will be so when God 'rises to terrify the earth' (Isa. 2:19, 21). Then, at the coming again of the Lord Jesus, a division will be made among the professing people of God (see Matt. 25; 1 Peter 4:17).

The psalmist's trepidation is to be related to the fact that while he could and did confess (as did others — see Hab. 3:17-19) that Jehovah was 'his' God (see v. 57), the expression 'My Father' as an address to God is completely absent from the pages of the Old Testament. Psalm 103:13 is the nearest approach to it. It is only the incarnation of the Son of God, the atonement he made on behalf of his people and the consequent witness of the adopting Spirit of God (see Luke 11:1, 13; Rom. 8:15-16; Gal. 4:4-6) that give an absolute assurance of being sons and daughters of the living God. The Lord God most high and holy is now *Abba* to each and every Christian (John 20:17). Even so, God is still God, and he is to be served 'with reverence and godly fear [because he] is a consuming fire' (see Heb. 12:28-29, NKJV). But perfected love has cast out that fear which is characterized by terror (see 1 John 4:17-19).

16.
TELLING THE TIME

Psalm 119:121-128

[121] I have done what is just and right;
   do not leave me to my oppressors.
[122] Give your servant a pledge of good;
   let not the insolent oppress me.
[123] My eyes long for your salvation
   and for the fulfilment of your righteous promise.
[124] Deal with your servant according to your steadfast
      love,
   and teach me your statutes.
[125] I am your servant; give me understanding,
   that I may know your testimonies!
[126] It is time for the LORD to act,
   for your law has been broken.
[127] Therefore I love your commandments
   above gold, above fine gold.
[128] Therefore I consider all your precepts to be right;
   I hate every false way.

There is something surprising about the first two lines of
this section. It is the fact that they contain no reference to
the Word of God. In that respect they are almost unique in

the psalm, verse 84 being the only other exception. This omission is of course deliberate on the part of the psalmist because his purpose is to focus attention on deeds, and not on words. He begins by saying, 'I have done ...', and then refers to what his adversaries intend to do. Next he tells the Lord what he wants him to do and again repeats what his adversaries are likely to do (v. 122). God's word is mentioned in the third line, but what the psalmist wants is for the Lord to do what he has said. Divine action is also highlighted in verses 124, where 'deal' is a translation of the verb 'do'. The same emphasis is expressed strikingly in verse 126. The final two lines record what the psalmist will do. The emphasis in this octet is clearly on deeds, not words.

Putting verses 121 and 126 together yields the following thesis: when the effect of God's word declared and obeyed by his people is minimal, it is time for God to do something more. This is what we shall use as a theme for the study of this section.

The Lord's act

As it is the divine name that is used here (see Exod. 3:13-16), this identifies the kind of activity the psalmist has in view. He is thinking of God's intervention as 'the LORD' in the exodus from Egypt. The work that is in view is salvation. It comprises both judgement of foes and mercy to his people. The psalmist is not thinking of either creation or providence, although it is only the one who created and who governs everything who could in fact be a saviour.

A kind of 'exodus' is therefore what the psalmist has in mind — but one that is to take place in Israel! Just as had happened in Egypt (Exod. 3:9), the 'insolent' in Israel 'oppress' the Lord's servants (see vv. 122, 124, 125). They in effect say, 'Who is the LORD, that [we] should obey his voice?' (Exod. 5:2).

The time

In verse 126 the psalmist is talking *about* the Lord and also *to* the Lord. In the first half of the line he speaks about the Lord, using the third person singular ('It is time for the LORD to act'); in the second half he addresses the Lord himself using the second person singular ('your', not 'his'). One seventeenth-century writer describes this as 'a polite suggestion', but it is hardly that, even with allowances being made for archaic language. The psalmist is being very bold and urgent, as he is in verse 84, which is also a request to God to act, and not only to speak!

In the course of his poem the psalmist has occasionally referred to others who fear the Lord (e.g. v. 63) and to himself as one who will instruct them (see v. 79). Here he is to be regarded as speaking to them and telling them the time. He is instructing them as to the severity of the situation, giving the reason for it, namely that God's covenant law has been annulled. The ESV translation needs to be stronger at this point. Although it is verbally accurate, its terms are too innocuous. What the psalmist is identifying is not that a specific command has been transgressed, or even several commands, but that the covenant itself has been broken (see Isa. 24:5; Jer. 11:10). He is telling those who know the Lord that they are living in a time of apostasy, and he wants all who fear the Lord to know it. Peter, John and Paul, the apostles of the Lord, do the same thing (see 2 Peter 3:1-7; 1 John 2:18-27; 1 Tim. 4:1-5; 2 Tim. 3:1-9). 'Seasons' of decline in the church and abounding evil in the world occur in that interval between the Lord's two comings which the New Testament identifies as 'the last days'. In such circumstances it is vital for Christians to know the time!

But he is also talking *to* the Lord because he did not write the consonants for '*his* law' but '*your* law'. It is as though an army of awakened intercessors has now been mobilized and they are telling the Lord the time and calling on him to act.

The expression used here does not mean that it is time for them to act for the Lord. That has been done by them, and by the psalmist, but the tide has not turned. The hour is late and the Lord needs to act. He is to be given no rest (Isa. 62:6-7; Luke 11:5-13). The psalmist longs for this deliverance (v. 123) and wants others to do so as well.

It was in this way that the 'true church' of the psalmist's day addressed the Lord in time of difficulty. They called on him as their forefathers did in Egypt (see also, for example, Ps. 78 – 80; Jer. 14:7-9, 19-22; Dan. 9). They did so with amazing boldness, calling on him to 'awake' and 'arise' ('wake' and 'get up'); to open his eyes and see; to open his ears and hear; to remember; to unfold his arms (cf. Ps. 74). The Lord does not mind being spoken to like this *provided that it is his believing servants who are doing so in desperate times*. The church at Jerusalem did much the same using Psalm 2 (see Acts 4:23-31). The Lord Jesus Christ instructed his disciples to address their heavenly Father like this by means of the second and third petitions of the Lord's Prayer:

Your kingdom come,
your will be done,
    on earth as it is in heaven

(Matt. 6:10).

The Exodus is the paradigm for the Christian salvation (Exod. 3:19-20; 6:6-8; Luke 1:51-55, 71-75; 9:31; Rev. 15:3). It is also the promise of intervention by the Lord to deliver his people from their foes in times of reformation and revival, which themselves are foretastes of heaven itself.

The Lord's timing

A great clash is pending in the psalmist's time. It is between those who, like him, have been doing what is just and right (v. 121) and the insolent, who have been doing evil (v. 115), rejecting the covenant (v. 126). The psalmist senses the approach of a point where the scales will be tipped in favour of injustice and unrighteousness. In verse 122 he uses an analogy from the law courts to describe this. It is as though he is being sued at law for unpaid debt and has no one to stand surety for him with regard to it, no one who would guarantee to pay in the event of his failure (see Prov. 11:15) and thus keep him out of prison, or from something worse.

Implicit in the kind of request that the psalmist is making for divine action, by way of a guarantee of legal immunity and protection (v. 122), fulfilment of a promise (v. 123), manifestation of covenant love (v. 124) and judgement of foes (v. 126), is a recognition that it is the Lord who decides whether and when to intervene. What may seem to his people to be 'the time' for him to act may not be so to him, for reasons best known to him, the one for whom a 'late' hour is never too late.

But the psalmist does not conclude this section with the magnificent request that we have been examining. Instead he ends it as he began, with a declaration of what he will do while he is waiting for an answer. He began by saying what he had done and he concludes by saying what he will do. He does not stop working because he starts praying. While he knows that divine intervention alone will meet the situation, he does not give up persevering in obedience. In fact what he says in the last two lines describes the very essence of true obedience. He speaks of 'love' that includes a practical, as distinct from a theoretical, understanding, one that has a moral effect, without which there is no fulfilling of the law (Deut. 6:5; Matt. 22:37; Rom. 13:8-10). Gold was regarded as the most valuable commodity at this time, but even gold could vary in quality. 'Fine gold' was the most rare kind, and consequently the most precious. But God's revelation of himself in his word surpasses it by far. Nothing therefore should replace God's word in the estimate of his people, and they should long for its fulfilment.

17.
THE WONDERFUL WORD

Psalm 119:129-136

[129] Your testimonies are wonderful;
   therefore my soul keeps them.
[130] The unfolding of your words gives light;
   it imparts understanding to the simple.
[131] I open my mouth and pant,
   because I long for your commandments.
[132] Turn to me and be gracious to me,
   as is your way with those who love your name.
[133] Keep steady my steps according to your promise,
   and let no iniquity get dominion over me.
[134] Redeem me from man's oppression,
   that I may keep your precepts.
[135] Make your face shine upon your servant,
   and teach me your statutes.
[136] My eyes shed streams of tears,
   because people do not keep your law.

From the way in which this section concludes (vv. 134, 136) it is clear that the psalmist's circumstances, as described in the previous section, have not significantly changed. He is still surrounded by those who break covenant with God and oppress his people, and no signal intervention in judgement and grace on the Lord's part has occurred in answer to his prayer. But he begins this section with the word 'wonderful', and that is an indication that his prayer has not gone unheard. His appreciation of the Lord's word has been increased, and so his devotion has not diminished. Even if the Lord does not choose to shatter the world, he strengthens his people (see John 14:22-24).

Wonderful

There are two dangers connected with this word, or rather with its use by Bible-believers today. The first is that many are carried away with an experience of wonder, rather than with what causes it; the second is that others (partly by way of an understandable reaction) empty the term of its experiential dimension. To pursue experience at the expense of truth presents a huge threat to the survival of orthodox Christianity; to think *only* of truth, and not experience, raises serious questions about the authenticity of orthodoxy. The appropriation of truth is never to be *equated with* either doctrine or experience, but with both.

The psalmist does not fall into either of these traps. He begins this section by describing God's testimonies (v. 129) and then continues by delineating their effects (v. 130-136). It is significant that he only uses the term 'wonder' in connection with God's words because it is they that take pride of place in authentic piety. We shall follow that line of thought in considering this section.

Wonders contained

As the opening word of this section is a plural noun, the translation could be: 'Wonders are your testimonies.' The noun 'wonder' is used in the Old Testament only for things divine, whether for God's words or for his deeds (Ps. 71:17; 72:18). By using it the psalmist is therefore confessing that the human words in which God's self-revelation had been expressed do not in any way impair their divine content. The human and the divine in Holy Scripture are not like oil and water, which do not mix, as some have thought; nor are they like wine and water, which do mix, but only to the detriment of the wine! Divine inspiration and human instrumentality combine perfectly so that neither ceases to be itself. God's word in human words is itself 'wonderful' and it is full of wonders.[1]

The Bible is therefore unlike, and superior to, every other book, whether Christian or not. Its ultimate author and subject matter are unique. In it God, who is incomprehensible and ineffable, speaks to his people about the one whose name is 'Wonderful Counsellor' (Isa. 9:6) and 'in whom are hidden all the treasures of wisdom and knowledge' (Col. 2:3). It is the true record of the 'great ... mystery of godliness' (1 Tim. 3:16).

Wonders unfolded

But the psalmist is aware that the wonders of God's word are not immediately obvious to all. In Israel there were the 'insolent' whose rejection of the word showed their ignorance of its truth and worth. But there were also those whom he describes as 'simple' (v. 130). This is wisdom language; the simple person is not 'the fool' by another name. 'The fool' is perverse, whether morally or intellectually or both; the simple is one who is easily impressed, whether for good or ill. The psalmist is therefore not categorizing all who do not fear the Lord and are not his servants (v. 135) as being 'insolent'. He also thinks of those who, though not adversely prejudiced, are not convinced either. They are gullible and need to be enlightened through the word (see Matt. 11:25).

The word that is translated 'unfolding' is only found here in the Old Testament. It is closely connected with the word for 'door' (see Gen. 4:7), and so 'opening' is appropriate. What is this 'opening', or 'unfolding'? Who does it, and how is it done? It is best to look in the rest of this psalm for an answer to these questions, and three places come to mind in that connection, namely verses 130, 102 (and v. 105) and 18.

1. *Verse 130.* In the second half of this line the psalmist declares that this 'opening' of God's words has an enlightening effect on people.

2. *Verses 102 and 105.* The emphasis here is on divine teaching. The 'opener' is therefore God himself.

3. *Verse 18.* The psalmist here acknowledges that there is a hindrance in him that acts like a blindfold, preventing him from seeing the 'wonders' in God's law.

The 'opening' referred to is therefore a divine activity. It results in the wonders that are in the word being displayed in such a way that they have an immense and lasting effect on the one whose mind is informed and whose heart is inflamed. Our Lord's ministry on the road to Emmaus is a perfect example of this and its effect (see Luke 24:28-35). This is what has been called the 'illumination', or 'internal testimony', of the Holy Spirit (see 1 Cor. 2:6-16; 2 Cor. 3:17-18). It can come about through means such as the preaching of the word,[2] the administration of the gospel ordinances, private and corporate Bible reading and prayer,[3] or apart from any means being used. But it always, *always,* leads to the truths of God's word, and never away from them (see 1 Cor. 4:6; 2 John 9).

The effects of this opening are identified in what follows in verses 131-136. The light that is referred to in verse 130 is the shining of the Lord's face on the soul through his word (v. 135; see also Num. 6:24-25). It is a spiritual sense of his favour.[4] This delight creates a longing for a continued sense of the Lord's presence in his word that is as intense as an animal's longing for water (v. 131; see also Ps. 42:1-2; 63:1-8) and leads to the prayer that the Lord will turn (his face) towards him (note the double 'me' in the first part of v. 132), according to his practice with regard to those who love his name.

But this truly spiritual delight does not make the psalmist unconcerned about either his conduct or his adversaries. Again he is concerned about his steps ('foot' is in the plural here unlike v. 105) and he wants to be kept free from sin's tyranny. So he pleads a promise that God has given to that effect (see also Ps. 19:13). He also believes that God can deliver him from the traps set by his opponents (v. 134), but he is not unfeeling about their plight. He sheds floods of tears for them on account of their refusal to turn to the Lord and keep his law (see Jer. 13:17; Lam. 1 – 5).

The great and staggering fulfilment of this statement is of course in the great grief of the Lord Jesus Christ (see Luke 19:41-44; Matt. 23:37-39). But the Lord's servants are also to share in this grief (see Rom. 9:1-5; Phil. 3:18-19).

18.
RIGHTEOUS, FAITHFUL AND LOYAL

Psalm 119:137-144

[137] Righteous are you, O LORD,
    and right are your rules.
[138] You have appointed your testimonies in righteousness
    and in all faithfulness.
[139] My zeal consumes me,
    because my foes forget your words.
[140] Your promise is well tried,
    and your servant loves it.
[141] I am small and despised,
    yet I do not forget your precepts.
[142] Your righteousness is righteous for ever,
    and your law is true.
[143] Trouble and anguish have found me out,
    but your commandments are my delight.
[144] Your testimonies are righteous for ever;
    give me understanding that I may live.

'Righteousness' is plainly what is uppermost in the psalmist's mind in this section. He refers to it five times in all, twice in each of two lines (vv. 137, 142) and also at the opening, the middle and the end. Found in those significant places, it is therefore the term that binds the section to-gether. Even so, the psalmist does not repeat it in a woodenly prosaic manner. He speaks of it by means of two closely related nouns, and not just one (vv. 138, 142), and he also employs an adjective for the purpose. More important than just a variety of terms is the fact that he not only speaks of the multi-faceted word in this way, but of the Lord himself, and he combines with it the reality of God's faith-fulness (vv. 138, 142). This combination of righteousness and faithfulness undergirds the Lord's word and his ways and it is what makes the psalmist loyal to God's truth in a time of great personal difficulty (vv. 141, 143). 'For ever' appears again in this section from verses 89-96.

Righteous

This adjective can be rendered 'upright' or 'straight' (v. 138 and perhaps v. 142), and conformity to a fixed standard is of the essence of its meaning. In the psalmist's time that standard was the covenant law that governed the Lord's relationship with Israel, her leaders and people. Priests and Levites, kings and judges were all to adjudicate in accord with it (see Deut. 17:8-20; Lev. 19:15; Deut. 25:1) and prophets were raised up to confront them and those they represented with the law in times of defection (Deut. 18:14-22). Amos used the image of a plumb line for this purpose as he brought the law of the covenant to bear on Israel, the apostate northern kingdom (see Amos 7:7-8). Isaiah did the same with Judah, predicting that the Lord would judge in accord with a plumb line of his justice and righteousness (see Isa. 28:17).

It is the Lord's 'rules', or judicial rulings, that are being spoken of. They are described as 'straight' — that is, the opposite of crooked. If it is the case that a king is speaking in this psalm, then we have a Davidic king declaring that all the Lord's rulings in the life of the nation, during his reign and prior to it, whether in judgement or salvation, have been in accord with covenant law and, what is more, that they cannot be otherwise because of the Lord's inherent righteousness. The Lord does not 'give way before the wicked' (see Prov. 25:26) and he does not forget his people (see Isa. 49:14-15). This is because it is against his nature to do so.

Faithful

The Lord's 'rulings' are also in accord with his testimonies (v. 138), which means that his judgements are in line with what he has prescribed in his law. The divine standard is not only fixed, but it has been made public and has been upheld. He made his testimonies known, commanding that they should be kept and committing himself to acting in accordance with them. There is not one law for the people and another for God. That is no basis for any relationship, let alone an abiding one, such as is indicated by the reappearance in this section of the word 'for ever', which is repeated in connection with both the Lord and his word (vv. 142, 144). That is most significant. The Lord cannot change (Mal. 3:6; James 1:17; Heb. 1:10-12) and his word is true (v. 142). He will not be inconsistent (see Num. 23:19). He cannot contradict himself. His sovereignty is not arbitrary. He can therefore be depended on — and he should be obeyed.

Just as there is no darkness of any kind in him, whether moral or mental, so there is none in his word. Using a metaphor borrowed from the process of refining dross from a precious metal ('well tried'), the psalmist declares that God's word is unalloyed. It is pure (see Ps. 12:6) and contains no foreign elements, whether of fact or of teaching. It is 'the truth, the whole truth and nothing but the truth'. Of course human beings do put God's word to the test (see Ps. 95:9;

Heb. 3:7 – 4:13), but that is not what the psalmist is referring to here. Because God's word of promise is not false the psalmist loves it. He has trusted in it in times of need and found that it held firm and proved good.

Loyal

The knowledge that God is always right and just in his words and deeds provides the psalmist with strength and joy, and so he declares himself anew to be the Lord's servant (v. 140). The Lord's unswerving consistency translates itself into zeal and ardour for God's praise and service. This is raised to such a pitch that it 'consumes' him; the verb means 'to bring to an end' (see comment on vv. 81-88) He has no strength left for anything else but to honour God!

The existence and activity of his foes (v. 139), the way in which he is dismissed and despised (v. 141) and the 'trouble' that causes him such 'anguish' (those two nouns are joined in the Hebrew to make one idea) are not overlooked, but they are outweighed by the precious and changeless words of the Lord (v. 143). Not only will he not forget them, but he will take delight in them (vv. 141, 143). Loving them with his mind and heart, he will obtain through them life that supplies invigoration for loyal and lifelong service (v. 144).

The loyal servant depicted here is a type of the Lord Jesus Christ, but also of all his servants. Zeal for the Lord's house consumed him (see Ps. 69:9, quoted in John 2:17). Surrounded by foes of God's word, he related to his righteous Father, finding delight in doing so (see Matt. 11:25-27; John 8:28-29). He confessed that God's word was truth (John 17:17). By his obedience in life and death he brought into being other servants (John 17:24-25) who boldly and gladly serve God as he did (Acts 5:41-42; 2 Cor. 4:7-16). And the God who can neither tempt nor lie (James 1:13; Heb. 6:18) will neither forget his servants' labour (see Heb. 6:10) nor excuse the harshness of his foes and theirs (see 2 Thess. 1:5-10). His faithfulness to them both fuels and sustains their faithfulness to him and to each other (see 2 Tim. 2:11-13; Heb. 10:32-39).

19.
NEAR BUT NEARER

Psalm 119:145-152

[145] With my whole heart I cry; answer me, O LORD!
    I will keep your statutes.
[146] I call to you; save me,
    that I may observe your testimonies.
[147] I rise before dawn and cry for help;
    I hope in your words.
[148] My eyes are awake before the watches of the night,
    that I may meditate on your promise.
[149] Hear my voice according to your steadfast love;
    O LORD, according to your justice give me life.
[150] They draw near who persecute me with evil purpose;
    they are far from your law.
[151] But you are near, O LORD,
    and all your commandments are true.
[152] Long have I known from your testimonies
    that you have founded them for ever.

The psalmist uses several terms in this section that continue into the next. There is his need for life (vv. 149, 156), the presence of persecutors (vv. 150, 157), his certainty of the Lord's loving kindness (vv. 149, 159) and, of course, the truth of God's word (vv. 151, 160). Those features are also found in earlier sections — see the uses of the verbs 'keep', 'guard', 'hope', 'meditate' and also 'call', which are prominent in this passage. This common vocabulary shows that the psalm is a harmonious poem but, more importantly, it indicates that piety has its own language and is a rounded life. The term 'for ever' also appears again.

Even so, there are words that appear here for the very first time as this verbal symphony draws to a conclusion. They are the words 'far' and 'near', which are used in two interconnected ways. First, the wicked, who are 'far from [God's] law' (v. 150), 'draw near' to the righteous. Secondly, the psalmist knows that the Lord is near to him, a representative of the righteous in Israel (v. 151). That is the picture drawn in the latter part of the section, while in the first we have the psalmist (the righteous) drawing near to the Lord (vv. 145-149). Perhaps James, the Lord's brother, had these verses in mind when he wrote, 'Draw near to God, and he will draw near to you,' after saying, 'Submit yourselves therefore to God. Resist the devil, and he will flee from you' (James 4:7-8). With these details in mind we shall work our way through this section.

The righteous draw near to the Lord

This is what is referred to in each of the first five lines. The psalmist repeats one and the same verb meaning 'call' (vv. 145, 146), but also employs some synonyms for it (vv. 147, 149). There is therefore repetition for emphasis and variation in the interests of style. Prayer is basic and vital. It is the way in which the righteous draw near to the Lord.

The psalmist's praying is lengthy. It covers a twenty-four-hour period beginning before daybreak (v. 147) and going on until the last watch of the following night (v. 148). It is a protracted cry for help (v. 147) because the need is great and a crisis is close at hand (v. 150). But it is also wholehearted and sincere (v. 145); it is not just an outburst because of difficulty. It is not only prompted by a need for deliverance or life (vv. 146, 149), but also by meditation on the Lord's words of promise (vv. 147, 148) that reveal his steadfast love and justice (v. 149; see also James 5:13-18). The psalmist therefore prays with hope as well as fervency. What he finds in the word is more than enough to turn into a day and a night of believing prayer (v. 147). These statements find an echo in the Lord's parables about the importunate friend (Luke 11:5-10) and the persistent widow (Luke 18:1-8). They are also borne out in our Lord's praying in the Garden of Gethsemane (Luke 22:39-53).

The wicked draw near to the righteous

The wicked approach the psalmist, not to join themselves to him in fellowship, much less to join themselves to the Lord in faith and repentance (Isa. 56:3,6-8), which is what they should do. They keep themselves as far away as possible from the law of the Lord that binds him and his people together, and in doing so they are distancing themselves from salvation (v. 155; see Acts 13:47).

Instead, their approach is made with the intention of putting into action a previously formed plan against the Lord's servant (see v. 110). It was an 'evil purpose' (v. 150), a word that is almost always associated with idolatry or immorality when it is used in the Old Testament. Ungodliness and unrighteousness are the twin pillars of sin. The plan of these persecutors therefore had connections with the covenant law of God, which forbade both. The psalmist was being accused of covenant-breaking by those who were themselves covenant-breakers, and there were many of them (see v. 157). This is what happened to Jesus the Messiah, who was treated as a blasphemer (Mark 14:55-65; John

10:33). Indeed, those who served his cause, like Jeremiah before him and Stephen after him, were also treated in this way (see Jer. 26; Acts 6:11-14). They and many others were all 'hated without a cause'.

The Lord draws near to the righteous

The divine name is used three times in this section[1] and so a covenantal character pervades its content. The psalmist's experience is like that of Israel in Egypt all over again — only here it is true Israel in the promised land needing the Lord's intervention against a false Israel. That is what lies behind the praying.

The opening of verse 151 is emphatic. It is a cry like the ones recorded earlier, but unlike them in that it is expressive of faith and joy. It is either the psalmist's response to the Lord's answer to his pleas (vv. 146, 149), or a testimony to it as the foes approach. The nearness of the Lord is therefore not spatial; it is relational. Yet it is none the less real. He makes his nearness known. The Lord hears the cry of his afflicted people and responds to them (see Exod. 6:5-8; v. 126). His presence is dynamic. His people frequently 'stand still and see the salvation of the LORD' (2 Chr. 20:17, NKJV). The result of this is that the psalmist can declare afresh what he had previously known and confessed about God's words, namely that they are stable and abiding (vv. 151, 152).

All this of course finds an echo in the thoughts and words of Jesus in his upper-room discourse (see John 14:30; 16:31-33) as he faced his adversaries and sought to prepare his disciples to face theirs too. He was accompanied by the Father (until the three hours of unspeakable and indescribable darkness and loneliness engulfed his soul) and assured his disciples that they would never be left as orphans in a hostile world. The cases of Stephen (Acts 6:13-14; 7:56-60) and Paul (2 Tim. 4:16-18), and the multitudes down the years who have suffered for his name's sake and righteous kingdom (see Matt. 5:10-11), demonstrate that the Good Shepherd does not leave the sheep when the wolf appears.

20.
GIVE ME LIFE

Psalm 119:153-160

[153] Look on my affliction and deliver me,
    for I do not forget your law.
[154] Plead my cause and redeem me;
    give me life according to your promise!
[155] Salvation is far from the wicked,
    for they do not seek your statutes.
[156] Great is your mercy, O LORD;
    give me life according to your rules.
[157] Many are my persecutors and my adversaries,
    but I do not swerve from your testimonies.
[158] I look at the faithless with disgust,
    because they do not keep your commands.
[159] Consider how I love your precepts!
    Give me life according to your steadfast love.
[160] The sum of your word is truth,
    and every one of your righteous rules endures for
        ever.

The expression, 'give me life,' is just one word in Hebrew and, although it does not begin with the consonant that introduces each line of this section, its use here is most significant. While the psalmist has used it before,[1] from verse 144 onwards he begins to use it more frequently, and it appears three times in this passage (vv. 154, 156, 159). This is another indication, besides those already mentioned at the beginning of the previous chapter, of a movement towards the poem's climax, and the psalmist's use of the word for 'sum' (v. 160) confirms this. But, more importantly, this triple plea for life makes it clear that a moment of grave crisis has arrived. The language of verse 153 connects with the previous section and enables one to say that the menacing approach of the wicked is now a reality. 'Life' is now an immediate necessity.

But what kind of life is needed? We have already seen in connection with previous uses of this term that the contexts in which it is found should be allowed to determine the kind of life that is being requested, whether it is physical or spiritual.[2] Given the nature of the threat presented in these sections, it can be said that 'life' should be thought of in as wide a sense as possible. It majors on the spiritual, but the physical aspect cannot be excluded. It is synonymous with 'salvation' (vv. 155, 166) and the fact that the psalmist asks for it means that the Lord is the one who gives it. Life can only come from the living God who is life-giving through Jesus Christ by the Holy Spirit. He is 'the LORD' (v. 126).

The appeal in verse 154 enables a finer point still to be put on this threat because it makes use of law-court language. To plead someone's cause is to act as a counsel for the defence. It is as if a trial is proceeding and the psalmist (the righteous) is in the dock. He has charges to answer and needs legal representation in order to secure their dismissal and his 'salvation'. The apostle Paul used the word 'salvation' with the same breadth of meaning as he awaited the outcome of his trial in Rome (see Phil. 1:19-25; 2 Tim. 4:16-18). We should also think of the Lord Jesus Christ, who was constantly having to face loaded questions and trumped-up charges, all of which combined in the 'evidence' that was submitted at his trial (see Mark 2:16-28; 12:13-27; Matt. 26:59-68).

The opening words of the other lines of this section introduce material that reinforces this plea for 'salvation'. The terms are 'look' (verses 153, 158, 159) and 'great', 'many' and 'sum' (vv. 156, 157, 160).

'Look' (or 'consider')

This is the psalmist's appeal to the Lord asking him to take note of his trouble (v. 153) and also of how he has regarded 'traitors in the camp' (see vv. 158-159). Formerly he asked the Lord to 'hear' (v. 149). Now he is asking the Lord to 'see'. No disrespect for the Lord is expressed by the psalmist in these bold requests to him to open his ears and eyes — though there may be when this kind of language is used in other settings and by other people (see Job 10:3-4; Mark 4:38-40). But the Lord is most understanding, patient and kind to his own!

The psalmist's words, however, are not only expressions of need, but also of confidence. He knows that the Lord is able both to hear and to see and, even more to the point, to act. In addition he is just (v. 153), faithful (v. 154), merciful (v. 156) and loving (v. 159). Such knowledge, however, only serves to increase the urgency when it seems that God has not taken any notice of those who love and serve him when they are in such trouble (see Ps. 74:18-20). Christians also addressed the Lord in this direct and confident spirit — 'And now, Lord, look upon their threats' (Acts 4:29; see also Acts 12:5) — and they may continue to do so.

'Great' or 'many'

Whenever a difference is made between what is quantitative and what is qualitative it is the former that is often preferred in our day. Numbers count! But the psalmist is not so taken up with the many adversaries that he cannot ascribe any kind of 'greatness' to the mercy of the Lord. In fact he gives pride of place to the Lord's mercy; he uses a plural noun, 'mercies', to refer to it. Mercy sees human beings as pitiable; grace sees them as guilty.

The psalmist lays hold of God's mercy because he is one against so many, or rather it is the other way round. He is to be pitied because he is in an unequal struggle and, what is more, it is an unethical one, for his opponents are wicked and treacherous, whereas he is righteous. But God's mercy and justice (see 'your rules' in v. 156) uphold and embolden him. The Lord loves those who love him (see Prov. 8:17). He honours those who honour him (1 Sam. 2:30). He delights to bring low those who exalt themselves and to raise up the downcast and weak (see 1 Sam. 2:1-10, especially vv. 4, 7-8; Luke 1:51-52).

So he concludes by speaking of 'the sum' of God's word being truth, and this term ought also to be connected with the idea of greatness. Apart from its literal meaning, which is 'head', it is a word that assigns prominence to someone or something among other associated items, and it is used in both a qualitative and quantitative way.

Qualitatively, it has a wide range of metaphorical uses referring to time (see Prov. 8:23; Num. 10:10) and rank, whether in the family (see Num. 1:4), the priesthood (see 2 Kings 25:18), or the army (Judg. 7:16, where the ESV translates it as 'companies'). A similar word is also used in the context of the description of wisdom (see Prov. 9:10).

Quantitatively, its use in connection with census-taking (see Exod. 30:12) indicates that it does not only refer to something general, but also to the specifics that comprise it, namely a head count.

'Sum' is therefore a good translation because it points to the fact that God's word is true both as a whole and in all its parts — its precepts and promises, statutes and judgements ('righteous rules' in v. 160). The psalmist is saying much the same as, 'How precious ... are your thoughts to me O God! How great is the sum of them!' (Ps. 139:17, NKJV) and the New Testament's declaration that 'exceedingly great and precious promises' (2 Peter 1:4, NKJV) are all 'Yes' and 'Amen' in and through Jesus Christ, to God's glory and the believer's comfort (see 2 Cor. 1:20-22). Not one of them will ever fail.

21.
JOY AND PEACE

Psalm 119:161-168

[161] Princes persecute me without cause,
    but my heart stands in awe of your words.
[162] I rejoice at your word
    like one who finds great spoil.
[163] I hate and abhor falsehood,
    but I love your law.
[164] Seven times a day I praise you
    for your righteous rules.
[165] Great peace have those who love your law;
    nothing can make them stumble.
[166] I hope for your salvation, O LORD,
    and I do your commandments.
[167] My soul keeps your testimonies;
    I love them exceedingly.
[168] I keep your precepts and testimonies,
    for all my ways are before you.

From the fact that the names of two letters appear above these verses (namely, *sin* and *shin*) it might seem as though this section of the acrostic employs two consonants, and not just one. That is not so, because the names are in reality two

slightly different pronunciations of the same consonant —
either 's' as in 'seat', or 'sh' as in 'shoot'. In this section there
are lines that begin with 's' (vv. 161, 162, 166), while the rest
begin with 'sh'. In the written text those sounds are distinguished by the location of a dot to the right or to the left
over the consonant, the form of which is also printed above
the text in some English translations. That little dot is (or
was) important — see the story in Judges 12 about 'shibbo-
leth' or 'sibboleth'!

There are no petitions in this section although persecution continues. But instead of requests there are expressions
of awe and joy (vv. 161, 162), love and praise (vv. 163, 164),
peace and safety (vv. 165, 166), and all of them are related to
willing obedience to the precious words of the Lord (vv. 167,
168). The section may therefore be described as the psalmist's profession of faith by way of response to the answers to
his prayers, uttered in the midst of the opposition that he
still faces.

But the psalmist does not express himself in only positive
terms. He gives vent to an abomination of 'falsehood'
(v. 163), and that word stands out in the original text because it begins with shin and is followed immediately by a
word that begins with sin. The psalmist could have switched
the order of those words in order to maintain the link with
the first two lines, which also begin with sin, but he chose
not to do so in order to highlight the word for 'falsehood',
which he declares that he 'hates' and 'abhors' (v. 163).

Falsehood

The word that is rendered 'falsehood' has a wide range of
uses in the Old Testament and usually it refers to more than
just the denial of what is factual. Truth is foundational for
life — both between man and man and also between man
and God. All truth is God's truth, after all is said and done.

Between human beings the term for 'falsehood' therefore refers to misrepresenting someone's name or misappropriating their goods (Hosea 7:1) in defiance of the eighth and ninth commandments (see Exod. 20:15, 16). Slander, theft and fraud, which undermine the stability of society, fall within its parameters. But 'falsehood' also figures in the higher relationship between human beings and God, for it vilifies the righteous (see vv. 78, 86); it is the stock in trade of false prophets (see Jer. 23:25, 26, 32) and is also the nature and effect of idol worship (Jer. 10:14). Deception, or what misrepresents and disappoints, is therefore of the essence of the term in this sense. Previously the psalmist has declared it to be futile (v. 118), but that does not mean that it has no power. The deception perpetrated in Eden involved distortion of God's word and his intention, and it resulted in 'death'. Lies have power.

What the psalmist is rejecting here is the equivalent of 'the devil and all his works', and he does so with vigour. He uses two verbs with a similar meaning — 'hate' and 'abhor' (v. 163; see also v. 104). Over against that he professes faithfulness to the Lord and his truth, and he does so in a spirit of devotion and a sense of duty to the Lord (v. 166) and his laws (vv. 167, 168). We shall now consider the couplets mentioned earlier.

Awe and joy

The psalmist has already referred to those who 'fear' the Lord (v. 79) and has also declared that God's word is of immense value, exceeding all earthly riches (vv. 14, 72). Here (vv. 161-162) he combines those responses, and he does so in an emphatic and graphic way. The word that is used for 'fear', or 'awe' (ESV), is a very strong one (see v. 120). It can mean terror. Here, however, it is devoid of any sense of dread, but describes a profound and all-pervading 'reverence and godly

fear' ('heart' is the core of the person). Although God stands
above his word, and that distinction is widespread in the
psalm, the psalmist regards God's word as worthy of no less
reverence than God himself. This is not 'worshipping a
book', as has often been sarcastically said. It is just recogniz-
ing 'the book' for what it is — 'the law of [God's] mouth'
(v. 72) — and this awe is connected with the boundless joy
of someone who finds a treasure amid the spoil after a battle
(v. 162; see also Matt. 13:45-46). The adjective 'great' reappears here from the previous section, and it will recur
(v. 165). It is used in a qualitative sense and functions as a
superlative.

Love and praise

Love (v. 163) and praise (v. 164) go together very naturally.
The first is the opposite of 'hate and abhor' (v. 163), and that
conveys something of its intensity. It expresses the vigour of
the mind, the affections and the will towards the Lord (see
Matt. 22:37-40) and therefore to his word, which 'always
tells it as it is', and will do so for ever (see v. 160). Such
affection is bound to translate itself into repeated and
unqualified praise. Seven is the number that symbolizes
completeness and perfection.

Peace and safety

The adjective 'great' figures once more, and this time it is
connected with 'peace' (v. 165). This is the only place in the
psalm where this word ('*shalom*') is used. It is a term that,
like others, defies adequate translation by any one English
word. In its most restricted sense it refers to silence; at its
widest it designates personal well-being in a perfect environment. The first use in the Bible of the 'big' words of the

faith often gives a clue as to how they should be understood. Using that idea, 'peace' is something promised by God that is entered into at death (Gen. 15:15). It is therefore supra-terrestrial and supratemporal. It belongs to eternity but it intrudes into time, and in this setting it describes the blessedness of knowing the Lord, loving his word and living in the light of it, in a fallen world. Such knowledge is a moment and a token of eternity. It is fittingly prefaced by the adjective 'great' because it describes and anticipates the heavenly. It provides a sure footing for a pilgrim in a hostile world and it is a foretaste of that 'salvation' for which the psalmist waits with expectation.

Meanwhile the psalmist lives *coram Deo* — that is, 'before' God (v. 168), and he does so by guarding and obey-ing the Lord's word out of a love that exceeds every other love (v. 167) but that is never excessive. It is not putting a higher regard on God's precepts and testimonies than they deserve, but giving him his due for his 'wonderful words of life'.

22.
PRAYER AND PRAISE

Psalm 119:169-176

[169] Let my cry come before you, O LORD;
    give me understanding according to your word!
[170] Let my plea come before you;
    deliver me according to your word.
[171] My lips will pour forth praise,
    for you teach me your statutes.
[172] My tongue will sing of your word,
    for all your commandments are right.
[173] Let your hand be ready to help me,
    for I have chosen your precepts.
[174] I long for your salvation, O LORD,
    and your law is my delight.
[175] Let my soul live and praise you,
    and let your rules help me.
[176] I have gone astray like a lost sheep; seek your servant,
    for I do not forget your commandments.

Prayers return in this final section and they predominate. But praise, lively praise, is not absent (see vv. 171, 172). The verb used in verse 172 can mean 'to sing', or 'to answer', and the one in verse 171 'to bubble up'. Those two lines can therefore be associated in terms of lively praise in song and, as the psalm is a poem, it does lend itself to being sung. (Its predecessors and successors in the Psalter certainly were sung and, what is more, 'meditation' was often done by means of chanting.) Even so, such praise might be the result of the psalmist's prayer (vv. 169, 170) having been answered. If that is so, then prayer predominates over praise even in those lines, and that sets up a most striking contrast with the last line, in which the psalmist confesses that he has strayed like 'a lost sheep' (v. 176). And that is the final note the psalmist strikes — or is it?

Verse 176 *is* the conclusion to this poem, but it hardly seems to be a climax. It may even cause perplexity or disappointment as there have been so many ringing crescendos of faith in the psalm — for example, in the previous section and even in this one (vv. 171, 172). But verse 176 is what the psalmist wanted as the last line of his magnificent poem.

And it is no anticlimax! The psalmist has not been building up a picture of sunlight without shadows and sweetness without bitterness in what he has written. That was not the character of the life of the godly either in the Old Testament or in the New, for that matter. What is said by happiness and prosperity merchants neither fits life in a fallen world nor life on earth as a prelude to life in heaven. There is no return to Eden as it was before the Fall and no heaven on earth by means of any self-help programme or religion, even the true one! What we have in the knowledge of God in Jesus Christ is only 'glory *begun* below'. The way to the Father's house is though a dark valley (Ps. 23:4). Zion is reached through the valley of weeping (Ps. 84:3-7) and the kingdom of God 'through many tribulations' (Acts 14:22).

The content of verse 176 does not therefore invalidate the positive declarations that we have seen in the preceding verses. Nor are they all hype and spin which need to be toned down in order to have some truth to them. Verse 176 is no more an anticlimax than it is an unrealistic climax.

What is it? It is sheer honesty; it is spiritual integrity — but in its own time and place in redemptive history, and that is how we shall consider it.

A straying servant

The expression 'lost sheep' in the first part of the line may cause difficulty because it seems to contradict all that the psalmist has said about himself in relation to the Lord. How can he be 'lost', given his prayers and praises? Another translation would be 'perishing', but that causes much the same difficulty. How can the author of this psalm be a lost, perishing sheep?

This question can be answered in two ways: first, by giving more attention to the verb 'wandered'; and, secondly, by noting that the psalmist describes himself as a 'servant'. With regard to the first, he has said previously, 'I went astray' (see v. 67) and has recorded that he had done so in a variety of ways. He has expressed a concern that he might not wander and has also acknowledged that he has done so (see vv. 5, 6, 10, 29, 35, 59, 101, 133). These verses show that what he thinks of as 'straying' is something as 'minimal' as being inwardly inconsistent, or even less than wholehearted in obedience, and not some flagrant and persistent way- wardness. Even so, this 'minimal' kind of wandering results in a loss of 'life' in its spiritual vigour, and that is what is depicted by the simile of 'a lost' or 'perishing sheep'. It is what he prays might be restored to him in the preceding line (v. 175).

But the psalmist does not only describe himself in that way. He also identifies himself as a servant of the Lord. This must not be overlooked. The one who says that he has wandered and is consequently declining, whether physically or spiritually, or both, declares that he is a servant of the Lord (v. 176; see also vv. 94, 125). He is therefore maintaining his trust in the Lord and has not renounced his word. He is someone who, having been found, is not 'lost' again in the sense that he was before!

This is a condition or need that characterizes all those who belong to the Saviour even in the era of the new covenant. Which Christians can be said (let no one dare to say!) to live up even to what they know, and to do so all the time — not to mention what is not known of the mind and will of the Lord that he has revealed in his word? The fact of inward conflict and outward disobedience is part and parcel of the life of those who have been born again. The flesh wars against the spirit in the Christian believer (Gal. 5:16-26). The Christian in the world is like 'sheep in the midst of wolves' (see Matt. 10:16), but is never 'sheep to be slaughtered' (see Rom. 8:36).

A seeking shepherd

Having described himself as a sheep, it is perhaps surprising that the psalmist does not address God as 'shepherd'. That of course is implied, but it is not stated in so many words. It would not be out of place in the context of Old Testament revelation had he done so (see Ps. 23; Isa. 40:11; Ezek. 34:11-16). But the fact is that the name 'LORD' includes this truth because it goes back to the Exodus deliverance when Israel knew that she had a King who had her well-being at heart and who was greater than Pharaoh. The psalmist therefore knows that in addressing God as 'the LORD' and owning that he is like a sheep he is effectively saying, 'The LORD is my shepherd.'

However, the really remarkable thing is that he asks the Lord to 'seek [his] servant' (v. 176), and nowhere else in this psalm does he do that. He frequently speaks about his need to seek the Lord and his precepts (see vv. 2, 10, 45, 94) and, by complete contrast, of the wicked as those who do not do so (v. 155). But only here does he ask the Lord to seek him, and that of course carries with it the inevitability of his being found and blessed with 'salvation' and 'life' (see vv. 173-175). He is convinced that the Lord has a shepherd's heart towards his people and that he will not leave them in distress, seeing that he has given them the promise of a Messiah, a shepherd-king (see Gen. 48:15-16; 49:24).

So this verse is a fitting conclusion to 'the Great Psalm'. True, it is not a climax, because nothing in the Old Testament can be that. But, like everything else from Genesis to Malachi, it can be called a 'pre-climax'! The psalmist's prayer was answered more abundantly than in either the deliverance from Egypt or the return from Babylon. It was the coming down to earth of the Good and Chief Shepherd, his going out into the wilderness of God's wrath so that he could gather each one of those the Father gave him to redeem (whether they lived before he came, like the psalmist, or afterwards) and his consequent gift of the Holy Spirit to each of them (see Gal. 4:4-7) so that they would be more confident and steadfast than even the psalmist and his fellow believers were.

And that is the best possible way to conclude an Old Testament poem — with an expectation of the coming of the Messiah and of the more abundant life that leads to the true climax, the consummation in glory where there will be no more wandering:

> For the Lamb in the midst of the throne will be their
> shepherd,
>   and he will guide them to springs of living water,
> and God will wipe away every tear from their eyes
> (Rev. 7:17).

NOTES

Introduction to Psalm 119

1. He was referring to the text of the old Latin version of the Bible.

2. Augustine, *Exposition of the Psalms*, Nicene and Post-Nicene Fathers, First Series, vol. 8, ed. Philip Schaff, Hendrickson Publishers, 1994, p.560 (translated from the Latin by E. A. Coxe).

3. See the many names mentioned in the introduction to W. S. Plumer's *Commentary on Psalms* (Banner of Truth Trust, 1975) and by C. H. Spurgeon in his *Treasury of David*; see also a selection of comments quoted at the end of the introduction.

4. David Noel Freedman, 'The Structure of Psalm 119' in *Pomegranates and Golden Bells: Studies in Biblical, Jewish and Near Eastern Ritual, Law and Literature in Honor of Jacob Milgrom*, ed. David P. Wright, David Noel Freedman and Avi Hurvitz, Eisenbrauns, Winona Lake, Ind., 1995.

5. See Will Soll, *Psalm 119. Matrix, Form and Setting*, Catholic Biblical Association of America Monograph Series 23, Catholic Biblical Association of America, Washington D.C., 1991, p.1.

6. He quotes the twentieth-century writers H. Gunkel and W. Buttenwieser to this effect.

7. Soll also quotes without disagreement a comment by Moses Mendelssohn, who described it as a 'series of incessant tautologies' in his commentary, *Die Psalmen*, F. Maurer, Berlin, 1783, pp.284-5.

8. John Calvin, *Sermons on Psalm 119*, Old Paths Publications, 1996, p.3.

9. John Calvin, 'To the Godly Readers', in his *Commentary on the Psalms*, vol. 1, ed. T. H. L. Parker, T. & T. Clark, 1965.

10. 'Acro' means 'high', as in 'acropolis', and 'stich' is a line or a part of a poetic line.

11. The same pattern is exhibited in Proverbs 31:10-31 and also in each of the first four chapters of Lamentations. Nahum 1:2-8 is half an acrostic.

12. Soll points out that some have thought that there are ten such nouns, and not eight. The extra ones are 'way' and 'truth' or 'path'. But those three are not used as often as the eight. They are therefore further descriptions rather than additional terms.

13. Derek Kidner, *Psalms 73-150*, Tyndale Old Testament Commentaries, IVP, 1975, p.417.

14. See Kidner, *Psalms 73-150*, p.416.

15. James Luther Mays, 'The Place of the Torah-Psalms in the Psalter', *Journal of Biblical Literature* 106/1 (1987), pp.3-12.

16. Serious questions have been raised about these since the middle of the last century by conservative Old Testament scholars. E. J. Young was aware of these, but was unwilling to give up the traditional understanding. In his *Introduction to the Old Testament* (published in 1953) he wrote, 'We are constrained to reject the position that the contents of the Psalms are often in conflict with the titles, and we believe that the titles are trustworthy indications of authorship.' The same was true of Derek Kidner. Since then volumes by R. K. Harrison, on the one hand, and Tremper Longman III and Ray Dillard, on the other, are much readier to pass these by as being non-original. Harrison wrote, 'The presence of superscriptions ... poses certain difficulties of historicity and interpretation' (p.977), but it may genuinely be doubted whether new *data* (i.e. post 1953) necessitate such a shift. A mediating position between Young and Harrison is taken by Mark Futato, who recognizes the titles as canonical but not factual-historical in *Interpreting the Psalms*, Kregel, 2007.

17. 'Pit' refers to a prison; cf. Jer. 38:7.

18. If a post-586 BC date for the psalm were to be established on other grounds, then Ezra, the scribe in the law of God, could qualify as a possible author.

19. Verse 46 refers to 'kings' and if it is Israel's monarchs who are in view here then that raises the possibility that the author was a

teaching priest in Israel or a prophet. But the reference could be to the kings of the surrounding nations.

20. See Andrew A. Bonar, *Christ and His Church in the Book of Psalms*, James Nisbet, London, 1859.

21. 'For the voice, that sweet voice, so well known to the ears of the Church, the voice of our Lord Jesus Christ and the voice of his body, the voice of the Church toiling, sojourning upon earth, living amid the perils of men speaking evil and of men flattering.'

22. J. A. Alexander, *The Psalms Translated and Explained*, Baker Book House, 1975, p.4.

23. See Geoffrey W. Grogan, *Prayer, Praise and Prophecy — A Theology of the Psalms*, Mentor, Christian Focus Publications, Fearn, 2001, p.7; J. Clinton McCann (ed.), *The Shape and Shaping of the Psalter*, JSOT 159, Sheffield. 1993; David Firth and Philip S. Johnston (eds.), *Interpreting the Psalms. Issues and Approaches*, IVP Academic, Illinois, 2005; G. H. Wilson. *The Editing of the Hebrew Psalter*, SBLDS, 76, Scholars Press, Chico, CA, 1985.

24. Kidner, *Psalms 73-150*, p.401.

25. Quoted in Plumer, *Commentary on Psalms*, p.1018.

26. Calvin, *Sermons on Psalm 119*, p.4.

27. Jonathan Edwards, *Treatise on Religious Affections*, Part 3, Section 3, *Works of Jonathan Edwards*, vol. 1, Banner of Truth Trust, Edinburgh, 1974, p.280.

28. E. W. Hengstenberg, *Commentary on the Psalms*, vol. 3, T. & T. Clark, 1876.

29. Alexander, *The Psalms Translated and Explained*, p.481

30. Charles Bridges, *An Exposition of Psalm 119*, Banner of Truth Trust, 1974, p.ix.

Chapter 1 — Blessed and blameless

1. The same root, but not the same word, opens the first two lines in the *Teth* (vv. 65-72) and *Kaph* (vv. 81-88) sections. See also the comment on verses 41-48 (*Waw*) in this regard.

2. Hebrew was originally written without vowels, and the consonants in this name are YHWH. The Hebrew people did not pronounce this name out of reverence, and so there has been great uncertainty as to how it is to be vocalized. *Yahweh* is the current scholarly consensus. *Jehovah* is the version of the name that is

more familiar to Christians because of its appearance in the KJV
and well-known psalms and hymns. This is the result of the
vowels from *elohim* being attached to the consonants YHWH.
3. Ps. 1:1; 2:12; 32:1, 2; 33;12; 34:8; 40:4; 41:1; 65:4; 84:4, 5, 12; 89:15;
94:12; 106:3; 112:1; 119:1, 2; 127:5; 128:1, 2; 137:8, 9; 144:15 (twice); 146:5.
4. See the translation of the psalm in *Word Biblical Commentary*,
vol. 2.
5. These psalms open Books 1 and 2 of the Psalter.
6. See the frequent use of the term in the Pastoral Epistles, e.g.
Titus 1:7.

Chapter 2 — From generation to generation

1. Rev. Philip Henry recommended it to his children in the seven-
teenth century. He advised them to 'Take a verse of Psalm 119
every morning to meditate upon, and so go over the psalm twice
in the year; and that, saith he, will bring you to be in love with all
the rest of the scripture; and he often said: All grace grows, as love
to the word of God grows.' The advice bore significant fruit in his
son Matthew, the well-known, much-loved Bible commentator
whose work is still widely read.
2. In later times Jewish boys participated in a ceremony called a
bar mitzvah when they undertook responsibilities to uphold the
law in the community.
3. See John Bunyan's *Holy War*.

Chapter 4 — Broad and narrow ways

1. Verses 104 and 128 contain similar thoughts but neither identical
words nor the same idiom; the translation 'every false way' is
accurate there, but not here.

Chapter 9 — The good, the bad and the better

1. Perhaps 'five' and 'one' in this sentence should be 'four' and 'two'
respectively, because the second part of the opening line is one
word short, an imbalance that could be made up by moving 'good'

from the beginning of verse 66 to the end of verse 65, where it would qualify 'word'. The acrostic arrangement would not be impaired by this transfer, because the word 'judgement' begins with the requisite consonant.

Chapter 17 — The wonderful word

1. Henry Martyn (1781–1812), who translated the New Testament into Hindustani and then into both Arabic and Persian, wrote, 'What do I not owe the Lord for permitting me to take part in the translation of his word? Never did I see such wonders and wisdom and love in the blessed book, as since I have been obliged to study every expression, and it is a delightful reflection that death cannot deprive us of studying its mysteries' (Martyn's *Life*, p.271, cited by Bridges, *Exposition of Psalm 119*, p. 334).
2. See the reference to Thomas Charles in note 4 below.
3. Jonathan Edwards wrote, 'I seemed often to see so much light exhibited by every sentence, and such a refreshing food communicated, that I could not get along in reading. I used often times to dwell longer on one sentence to see the wonders contained and yet almost every sentence seemed to be full of wonders.'
4. After hearing Daniel Rowland preach on Hebrews 4:15, Thomas Charles wrote, ' I had such a view of Christ as our High Priest, of his love, compassion, power and all-sufficiency, as filled my soul with astonishment — with joy unspeakable and full of glory. My mind was overwhelmed and overpowered with amazement. The truths exhibited to my view appeared too wonderfully gracious to be believed. I could not believe for very joy. The glorious scenes then opened to my eyes will abundantly satisfy my soul millions of years hence in the contemplation of them' (*The Calvinistic Methodist Fathers of Wales*, trans. John Aaron, Banner of Truth Trust, Edinburgh, vol. 2, p.242).

Chapter 19 — Near but nearer

1. Eight of the twenty-three uses are found in the last six sections of the psalm. Prior to them the previous sixteen sections contain the remaining fifteen occurrences.

Chapter 20 — Give me life

1. The first occurrence is in verse 25. Derek Kidner surveys its uses most helpfully in his work on *The Psalms*. He writes, 'Sometimes the link between Scripture and the gift of life consists of a promise which the singer claims (vv. 25, 50, 107, 154); sometimes it is that the very keeping of God's laws is restorative (v. 37) and life-giving (v. 93) ... since they turn one's eyes and steps towards Him. Sometimes, conversely, the psalmist asks for life to enable him to keep these precepts (v. 88 and perhaps v. 40).'

2. It is an advantage that the ESV translates it in exactly the same way whenever it occurs in the psalm.

Also by Hywel R. Jones

An ⊕ Study Commentary

JOB

HYWEL R. JONES

ISBN 978 085234 664 8

The book of Job has been highly spoken of by many, both inside the Christian church and out. Thomas Carlyle, the nineteenth-century man of letters, wrote of it, 'I call it ... one of the grandest things ever written with pen... There is nothing written, I think, in the Bible or out of it, of equal literary merit.' Martin Luther described it as 'magnificent and sublime as no other book of Scripture'.

As a part of Holy Scripture, it is imbued with a far higher inspiration than any one of the world's great classics. By it, God aims to instruct and encourage his people in their earthly pilgrimage towards heaven, just as he does in all the other books of the Bible. But, as Hywel Jones ably demonstrates in this commentary, the breadth of its appeal also means that it supplies excellent material for evangelism. Set outside the life of Israel, the book of Job provides a ready-made point of contact with unchurched people. There are so many who have lost their way, either because they do not ask the big questions about life, or because they are swamped by the fact that there seem to be no real answers to them. By its presentation of both the grim realities of human existence and the wonder of divine grace, the book of Job has something to say to people of every culture and every age who are prepared to consider it seriously.

'The Great Psalm' (Psalm 119) was written for the whole of life. It therefore takes a whole lifetime to be equipped to expound it well and apply it wisely. Enter Dr Hywel Jones — teacher, author, pastor — much loved by his seminary students and colleagues, and esteemed by those who are privileged to be among his friends. In his hands the precious jewels are well mined. This beautiful exposition comes from a lifetime of taking in and giving out God's Word. Its hallmark is the careful, thoughtful and richly spiritual unfolding of divine wisdom. Both a pleasure to read, and a treasure to share.

Sinclair Ferguson

The announcement that Hywel Jones is expounding God's Word in devotions at our seminary arouses special interest and expectation. Although he possesses admirable personal qualities, it is his consistent attention to the grain of each passage that is so rewarding. If Psalm 119 celebrates God's Word, then I can think of no better celebrant than Hywel Jones.

Michael Horton
J. Gresham Machen Professor of Systematic Theology and Apologetics, Westminster Seminary California

Sales of this book help to promote the missionary work of EP in making good Christian literature available at affordable prices in poorer countries of the world and training pastors and preachers to teach God's Word to others.